THE CONSEQUENCES OF CHAOS

Çok sevgili Benan'a,

Seminerimize katıldığınız

için teşekkürlerimle,

Kemal

24 Mayıs 2016

D1059740

THE MARSHALL PAPERS

After World War II, Brookings scholars played an instrumental role in helping the United States craft a concept of international order and build a set of supporting institutions, including what became known as the Marshall Plan, in honor of Secretary of State George C. Marshall who spearheaded the effort. Now, a generation later, the Brookings Foreign Policy program has evoked that vital historical juncture by launching The Marshall Papers, a new book series and part of the Order from Chaos project. These short books will provide accessible research on critical international questions designed to stimulate debate about how the United States and others should act to promote an international order that continues to foster peace, prosperity, and justice.

THE MARSHALL PAPERS

THE CONSEQUENCES OF CHAOS

SYRIA'S HUMANITARIAN CRISIS AND THE FAILURE TO PROTECT

ELIZABETH FERRIS
AND KEMAL KIRIŞCI

BROOKINGS INSTITUTION PRESS
Washington, D.C.

Copyright © 2016
THE BROOKINGS INSTITUTION
1775 Massachusetts Avenue, N.W., Washington, D.C. 20036
www.brookings.edu

Library of Congress Cataloging-in-Publication data are available.

ISBN 978-0-8157-2951-8 (pbk)
ISBN 978-0-8157-2952-5 (e-book)
9 8 7 6 5 4 3 2 1

Typeset in Minion

Composition by Elliott Beard

Contents

Foreword

The international order is in trouble. For a quarter century, the world has experienced growing global interdependence largely characterized by the absence of geopolitical competition and the leadership of the United States. Now there are several, possibly fundamental, challenges to that order—in Asia, where the rapid rise of China is disrupting relationships across the region; in Europe, where Russia seeks to undo the post–Cold War settlement through aggression; and in the Middle East, where the regional state system itself is breaking down and we have entered a phase of bloody regional competition and a geopolitical proxy war.

The return of geopolitics has been accompanied by a return to competition between democracies and autocracies. China's rise and Russia's recovery have generated a new model of "authoritarian capitalism." This comes at a time when the global financial crisis has put a dent in the credibility of the Western economic model, and the disappointments and consequences of the Arab Spring have led many to question the value of promoting liberal democracy. It also comes amid relative weakness in the Western alliance system, characterized by political nativism in Washington, double- or even triple-dip recession in Europe, and continuing economic stagnation in Japan.

Transnational and global threats also pose deepening challenges both to the United States and its geopolitical competitors. Climate change, pandemic disease, and jihadist terrorism illustrate the human cost and potential risks of weak states in the international order.

All told, we appear to be at one of history's pivotal junctures, and again the response of the United States will be critical. For all the talk of America's relative decline, the United States retains more capacity than any other power to impact the calculations and policies of others. But America's competitors are too powerful and their visions too different to imagine that U.S. leadership alone is a sufficient ingredient to maintain the liberal, rules-based international order that now feels so threatened.

In short, the task is urgent and complicated: how to reinvent the liberal international order in the face of so many centrifugal, chaotic forces so that it can provide greater stability, peace, prosperity, and freedom; and how to do it in ways that encourage cooperation from other world powers, reduce friction generated by competition with them, and if necessary contain or constrain their ability to undermine the order.

For these reasons, Foreign Policy at Brookings has launched a two-year project on "Order from Chaos" with three core purposes: to analyze the dynamics in the international system that are creating stresses, challenges, and a breakdown of order; to define U.S. interests in this new era and develop specific strategies for promoting a revitalized rules-based, liberal international order; and to provide policy recommendations on how to develop the necessary tools of statecraft (military, economic, diplomatic, and social) and how to refashion the architecture of the international order.

At an earlier juncture in history, as the Second World War came to a close, Brookings played an instrumental role in helping the United States craft a concept of international order and a set of supporting institutions. The highlight of this was a Brookings-drafted program that was introduced by Secretary of State George C. Marshall and became known as the Marshall Plan.

It is to recall that moment and invoke its spirit—the application of policy research to the crafting of effective international strategy—that the Order from Chaos project has chosen to initiate The Marshall Papers. Their purpose is to provide accessible, long-form research on critical international questions designed to stimulate debate about how the United States and others should act in the world to promote international order—an order that adapts to new realities to be sure, but one that continues to foster peace, prosperity, and justice. That is the foreign policy challenge of our time, and the connecting theme of these papers.

BRUCE D. JONES
Vice President, Foreign Policy
Brookings Institution

Preface

A humanitarian catastrophe—a tide of refugees fleeing Syria—is now entering its sixth year and the international community is still struggling to respond. The resources of the governments hosting the refugees, aid agencies, nongovernmental organizations, and a multitude of other actors are being tested. In the absence of viable political solutions to the conflict, governments in the region and the broader international community are all struggling to respond to the humanitarian needs of Syrian refugees and internally displaced persons (IDPs). No final solution to the war in Syria appears in sight and funds to support an ever-increasing population of displaced persons are neither sufficient now nor likely to be sustainable in the future.

The Syrian situation is occurring against the background of a global crisis of displacement. According to the United Nations High Commissioner for Refugees, in 2014 almost 60 million people have been forced from their homes by conflict, violence, and persecution. Furthermore, a large proportion of these people have been uprooted for a very long time. Finding solutions for long-term displacement has long been on the global humanitarian agenda, but the international community is failing in this task, especially in terms of resettling refugees and providing adequate funding for humanitarian assistance.

All trends point to Syria becoming yet another long-term, intractable displacement crisis with profound implications for Jordan, Lebanon, and Turkey, the major host countries for Syrian refugees, as well as the EU and the broader international community. Can something be done about it?

In any attempt to address this question it is important to recognize the implications of the Syrian displacement on the current international order. The Syrian conflict and resulting displacement are clear signs that the present international system for preventing and resolving conflicts has been deeply challenged—at least in the Middle East. The Syrian displacement is also a clear indictment of the limitations of the United Nations as well as regional bodies to prevent and resolve such crises. Ultimately, the solution to the Syrian IDP and refugee crisis is political and demands an end to the violence and destruction in Syria. Only during the course of the last months of 2015, as the conflict in Syria began to affect the international security and stability of Europe, have any high-level efforts been launched to address the root cause of displacement. Meanwhile, the challenge of extending humanitarian assistance and protection to displaced Syrians continues to call for burden sharing and international solidarity.

It is no secret that an interrelationship exists between political and diplomatic solutions to the Syrian conflict and remedies to the displacement crisis. It is critical that as efforts geared to solve the Syrian conflict gather momentum, the international community consider the effects of such solutions on resolving displacement. First, any political resolution needs to incorporate terms and provide sufficient funds for both physical reconstruction of the country itself and support Syrians who wish to voluntarily move back to their communities. This is likely to take years. Second, any remedy to the Syrian conflict will need to be accompanied and sustained by processes of reconciliation if returns of refugees and internally displaced persons are to be sustainable.

In the meantime, addressing the current displacement crisis should be based on recognition of at least two important realities. First, refugees themselves are actors capable of taking their own destiny into their hands—as demonstrated in their mass movement out of the region in the past year. While refugees and IDPs are usually depicted in Western media only as victims of conflict, they are survivors.

Second, it is important to bear in mind that the burden of protecting and assisting refugees has largely fallen on the shoulders of major host countries—primarily Jordan, Lebanon, and Turkey. The governments of these countries are providing a public good for the international community, and it is indeed disappointing that appeals by host governments and the UN system for more assistance received scant attention—until large numbers of Syrians began to arrive in Europe. Finally, as the European refugee crisis is making increasingly clear, it is in the best interest of the international community and Europe that a new formula be found for effective burden sharing with these host countries.

It is against such a background that in *Consequences of Chaos* we propose a New Global Approach for Syria. The development of this approach would bring together the governments of refugee-hosting countries, the UN and other intergovernmental agencies, regional bodies, international nongovernmental organizations and local civil society actors, and donor governments to consider and adopt a new system of burden sharing. The focus would be centered around

- Reaffirming the principle that protection of refugees is an international responsibility;
- Supporting common legal and policy approaches to Syrian refugees in the region that includes access to livelihood opportunities;
- Reaffirming resettlement as a core component of refugee protection and assistance and retooling elements of resettlement policy to meet the needs of especially the most vulnerable of refugees;
- Providing a forum for creative thinking on solutions for internally displaced people;
- Establishing a new relationship between humanitarian and development actors;
- Engaging development actors such as the World Bank more effectively; and
- Laying the groundwork for longer-term reconstruction and recovery efforts in Syria.

The process of developing this New Global Approach for Syria could be worked out through a consultative process with stakeholders over a six-to-twelve-month period jointly led by the UN secretary general and the president of the World Bank and could culminate in a global meeting in March 2017. Then, the challenge would be for executive bodies to actually implement these policy recommendations. The New Global Approach for Syria, if successfully implemented, would offer a "win-win" outcome, foremost, for Syrian refugees and IDPs, but also for major host countries as well as the EU, not to mention the broader international community. This new system combining relief and humanitarian assistance with a developmental approach may form the skeleton of a template for managing the broader global refugee crisis as well as help reform international humanitarian governance.

Acknowledgments

We are grateful to the Director's Special Initiative Fund (Foreign Policy at Brookings) for supporting this research, to Sarah Drury and Sinan Ekim for their research assistance, to Sema Karaca for her help in arranging field research in Turkey, and to the refugees, government officials, and staff of humanitarian organizations who spoke with us about their experiences.

CHAPTER 1

The Context, Causes, and Consequences of Syrian Displacement

The displacement of almost 13 million Syrians—half the country's population—is the most daunting humanitarian crisis of our time. In the absence of viable political solutions to the conflict, governments in the region and the broader international community are all struggling to respond to the humanitarian needs of Syrian refugees and internally displaced people (IDPs). Political actors, unable to agree on how to end the violence, agree that humanitarian assistance is needed, but the funds are neither sufficient now nor likely to be sustainable in the years ahead. The conflict that is driving the displacement has become more complex over the past few years, particularly with the proliferation of actors involved, and solutions appear more elusive than ever. As starkly illustrated by the November 2015 Beirut and Paris attacks, Syria's humanitarian crisis has implications not only for Syrian civilians but also for the course of the conflict, governments in the region, governments beyond the region, the international humanitarian system, and indeed for global peace and security.

While dozens of articles and studies have looked at the scale of the Syrian displacement crisis, this book takes a step back to look at the larger issues raised by the Syrian crisis and in particular its implications for global governance.

THE GLOBAL CONTEXT: IT'S NOT JUST SYRIA

At the present time, humanitarian actors are struggling to respond to multiple mega-crises. The number of displaced persons has reached levels not seen since the end of World War II. Worldwide, almost 60 million people have been forced from their homes by conflict, violence, and persecution (figure 1-1). While Syrian displacement is the most visible manifestation of this trend, it is far from the only case. And the rarely acknowledged fact behind these numbers is that most of the world's 60 million refugees and internally displaced people have been uprooted for a long time. The global displacement crisis is as much about the failure to resolve long-term displacement as about new conflicts displacing millions of people. Some 60 percent of the 60 million uprooted have been displaced for more than five years, and refugees, on average, have been uprooted for seventeen years.[1] Finding solutions for long-term displacement has long been on the global humanitarian agenda, but the international community is failing in this task. In 2015 the fewest number of refugees returned to their countries than at any time since 1983.[2]

Right now, there simply are too many simultaneous mega-crises: Syria, Iraq, Yemen, and Libya in the Middle East; Ukraine; South Sudan, Burundi, and Central African Republic; Afghanistan, Nepal, and the Rohingya in

FIGURE 1-1. *Number of People Displaced by Conflict, 2005–14*

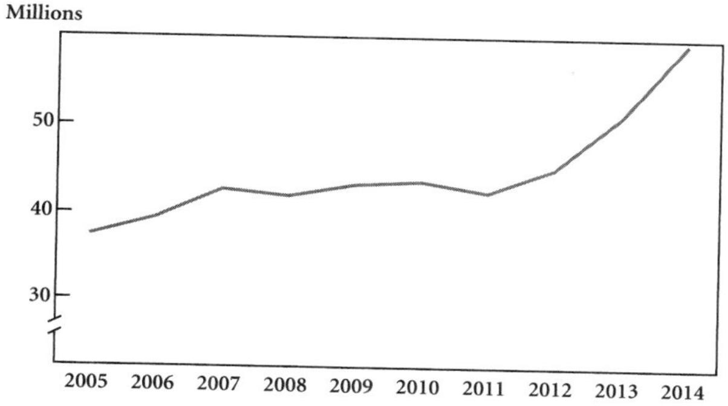

Millions

Source: United Nations High Commissioner for Refugees.

Myanmar. There are also displacement crises in Colombia, Central America, and Mexico; still-fragile situations in Mali, Somalia, Eritrea, and the Sahel; lingering effects of the Ebola crisis in West Africa; and the continuing saga of deaths in the Mediterranean. Humanitarian actors are scrambling to respond to all of these crises. Not only is humanitarian funding under pressure, but there is a shortage of experienced humanitarian staff and a lack of creative and critical thinking about the larger issues beyond the immediate crises. International attention is fickle and gravitates to the crisis of the day, moving away from protracted crises even though people remain displaced and in need.

Today's humanitarian crises are a reflection of changing patterns of violence and conflict. Overall trends indicate that the world is much less violent than during the Cold War and its immediate aftermath. In fact, most regions of the world have seen reductions in levels of violence over the past twenty years. While data from the Uppsala Conflict Data Program show that over 100,000 people were killed in organized violence in 2014—the highest rate of fatalities in twenty years—this is still much lower than the previous peak in 1994.[3] However, the last five years have seen an upsurge in organized violence, particularly in the Middle East, where a combination of weak national states, corrupt economies, and Western passivity has led to what Peter Harling and Alex Simon have called the "chaotic devolution of power" and the "militiarization" of societies.[4] While the roots of the Syria conflict are clearly in the political and economic failures in the region, the international system has been unable to prevent the escalation of the conflict, in spite of the endorsement by the UN World Summit of the concept of Responsibility to Protect in 2005.[5]

If the international community cannot develop the means to prevent and resolve the conflicts that displace large numbers of people, as in Syria, then it needs to invest more in supporting solutions for refugees and IDPs and others suffering the effects of those conflicts, including host communities. If successful, such efforts could also serve as models for other seemingly intractable conflicts that have displaced millions, as in Iraq and Yemen. Such initiatives, as discussed in the concluding chapter of this study, could include more support and different kinds of support for refugees in neighboring countries and for resettlement in more distant lands as well as using development assistance to support solutions for refugees and IDPs. Rather than paying large (though insufficient) sums of money to support care and maintenance programs for Syrian refugees, perhaps greater incentives should be offered to host governments to support long-term integration of refugees into their countries.

There also may be ways to do much more to recognize the agency of refugees and IDPs themselves and support their efforts to find their own solutions to displacement. As discussed below, most of the Iraqi refugees who fled their country in the mid-2000s have likely found their own solutions, without international support. Oxford University researchers have deemed this "accommodation" rather than integration.[6] Host communities need to be reassured that the presence of refugees can contribute to economic growth if they are given a chance to help themselves. Furthermore, their "accommodation" need not mean discouraging them from returning home. If anything, recent research suggests that economically better integrated refugees are more likely to more successfully manage the return process when the time comes.[7]

Ideas and recommendations are spelled out more fully in the concluding chapter, but the authors want to signal from the beginning that the Syrian displacement crisis compels the international community to look beyond short-term humanitarian solutions. The Syrian crisis—coming as it does on top of too many other mega-crises—is a clear sign that the international humanitarian system can no longer cope. The only answer is not simply for Western governments to pony up more money for more relief aid for Syrians displaced for decades to come. Nor is it to bring more donors—such as China and the Gulf states—into the existing system (though that is certainly needed to address current shortfalls). The magnitude of the crisis and the scale of human suffering compel the search for bold and even radical solutions for the failures of our present global system.

THIS BOOK

This study begins by placing the Syrian displacement crisis in the context of the Middle East—a context shaped by poor governance, violence, and resulting waves of displacement that have influenced the region's response to Syrian refugees and IDPs. This is followed by a short overview of the now-familiar ground of the descent of Syria into civil war with an emphasis on the conflict's effect on displacing people. The particular impact of the refugee flows on Syria's neighbors—Jordan, Lebanon, and Turkey—is then considered with analysis of how these three countries have tried to cope with the situation in the face of inadequate burden sharing by the international community. Discussion then turns to the more recent phenomenon of Syrian refugees making their way to Europe and the impact of this flow of refugees not only on Europe and the global humanitarian architecture but indeed on international peace and security too. Chapter 3 addresses some of the challenges posed by those displaced—and trapped—inside Syrian borders. While protecting and assisting Syrian refugees in host countries is a mammoth task, the challenge of doing so for those displaced within Syrian borders is even more daunting. Finally, the book concludes with a chapter analyzing the identified trends and suggesting possible ways forward. Solutions for resolving Syria's civil war are not presented, except in passing to note their possible humanitarian consequences. However, it goes without saying that ultimately finding solutions for those displaced will require addressing the very root cause of the crisis: the war in Syria.

This study is based on field researches carried out since 2013 in Jordan, Lebanon, and Turkey and on dozens of interviews with humanitarian actors, including those working inside Syria and in Iraq.[8] Most of those writing about Syrian displacement focus on the numbers. Numbers are important, but they are constantly changing. The figures presented here are current as of the end of 2015, and it is likely that these figures will be out-of-date before this book is even published. But the issues around Syrian displacement are much broader than the number of people displaced on a given date, and this study seeks to look beyond the numbers to the larger trends and political implications of Syrian refugee and IDP flows.

A word on definitions: A refugee is a person who has crossed an internationally recognized border because of conflict or persecution. Protection of refugees is guaranteed under the 1951 Refugee Convention and 1967 Protocol.[9] Neither Lebanon nor Jordan has signed this treaty. Although Turkey has ratified the Convention, it maintains a geographical limitation, restricting formal refugee status to Europeans. In this paper, the term "refugee" is used to refer to Syrians who have fled to other countries since the conflict broke out in 2011, whether or not recognized as such by the host governments.

The definition of an internally displaced person is much broader and carries less legal weight. Unlike refugees whose rights are upheld in a long-established, legally binding convention, the normative framework for IDPs is much more recent and much less formal. *The Guiding Principles on Internal Displacement,* although affirmed as an important framework by the 2005 World Summit, are not a legally binding international treaty.[10] While the United Nations High Commissioner for Refugees (UNHCR) is mandated to protect and assist refugees, there is no corresponding international organization responsible for IDPs; rather, that responsibility lies with national authorities, supported at times by a looser system of international agency involvement. Globally there are around three times as many IDPs as refugees.

THE MIDDLE EAST CONTEXT

While unusual in its intensity and its direct impact beyond the region, the Syrian refugee crisis is just the latest of a long series of large-scale displacements of people in the Middle East over many centuries. Two of the most recent displacements—of Palestinians after the founding of Israel and of Iraqis during and after the rule of Saddam Hussein—provide particular context for understanding the plight of Syrians today, including the treatment of them by neighboring countries.

The Ongoing Palestinian Legacy

In 1948 some 700,000 Palestinians (95 percent of the total Arab population in the area) fled or were forced from their communities and have largely lived as refugees ever since.[11] This displacement not only shaped Palestinian identity, but it has dominated Arab-Israeli relations for sixty-plus years and has influenced the region's response to later waves of displacement, including both Palestinian and Iraqi refugees. In 1948 the assumption was that the influx of Palestinian refugees would be a temporary phenomenon. The UN Conciliation Commission for Palestine was established in 1948 to mediate the conflict; it failed to do so (a long and fascinating story) and ceased its protection functions in the mid-1950s. A successor agency, the United Nations Relief and Works Agency for Palestinian Refugees in the Near East (UNRWA), was created in 1950 with a three-year mandate but is still with us today, caring for almost 5 million Palestinian refugees, including 2 million in Jordan and about half a million each in Lebanon and Syria (before the outbreak of the Syria conflict in 2011).[12]

In light of the present Syrian crisis, it is interesting and sad to look back at the early history of the international response to the plight of Palestinians. Sometimes there is an assumption that certain bits of history are all preordained, but other outcomes were in fact possible back then. The fact that a separate UN agency was created to deal with Palestinian refugees (rather than including them in UNHCR, which was also established in 1950), that the UN Conciliation Commission was disbanded, that more than fifty camps were set up for Palestinians, that the right of return was enshrined in UN resolutions, and that Arab governments found it useful to maintain the visibility of the refugees as a bargaining chip with Israel—together meant that solutions to Palestinian displacement would remain elusive. At least some of these factors are also at play in the current Syrian refugee crisis.

The long-term presence of the Palestinian refugees has shaped host governments' response to both the Iraqi and Syrian refugees in several ways. Lebanon and Jordan welcomed the Palestinian refugees in 1948, expecting that their presence would be a temporary phenomenon. Nearly seven decades later, the Palestinian population in the region has increased more than fivefold. Lebanon and Jordan took different paths in their treatment of the Palestinians. While Jordan gave Palestinians the right to become citizens (and most UNRWA-registered refugees in Jordan have done so), Lebanon kept citizenship off the table out of concern for its own fragile sectarian balance (although Lebanon did grant citizenship to about 50,000, mainly Christian, Palestinians in the 1950s). It was not until 2010 that Palestinians in Lebanon were allowed to work on the same basis as other foreigners (although the process is onerous and they are still prohibited from working in some 20 professions).[13] Syria, in fact, was one of the host countries most accepting of Palestinian refugees.

Several lessons from the experience of Palestinians are relevant to our story of Syrian refugees today. Governments of host countries recognized that allowing refugees to stay temporarily was no guarantee that they would soon leave. Today, Lebanese and Jordanians constantly draw parallels between the Syrian and Palestinian situations. "We thought our Palestinian brothers and sisters would only stay for a short time," one Lebanese official noted. "They've been here 67 years. We won't make that mistake again." Another official said: "If we make life too easy for them, they'll never find solutions elsewhere."[14]

Local integration of Syrians—the second so-called durable solution for refugees—is off the table for discussions in Jordan and Lebanon.[15] Giving refugees the right to work or to become more self-reliant is seen as opening the door to allowing them to stay indefinitely, which after the Palestinian experience is simply not acceptable. The long-standing Palestinian presence was also a factor in the refusal by governments in the region to ratify the 1951 Refugee Convention (or, in the case of Turkey, maintaining the geographical limitation). Why take on more legal obligations when they were already hosting large numbers of Palestinians?

Other impacts of the Palestinian situation have been a reluctance to establish camps that might turn into permanent settlements along with a tendency to view Palestinian refugees themselves with suspicion. When Iraqi refugees began fleeing in the mid-2000s (more on this below), Jordan and Syria generously allowed them to enter—except for the Iraqi Palestinians who were confined to no-man's land areas between the borders until they were eventually resettled elsewhere. Again when the Syrian refugees began to pour across the border of neighboring countries, Jordan imposed restrictions on the entry of Palestinians, followed in May 2014 by Lebanon. Difficulties for Palestinian refugees entering Turkey were also reported.

And Then There's Iraqi Displacement

Iraqi refugee movements have a long and volatile history, with multiple displacements (both internal and cross-border) during the Saddam Hussein regime (1979–2003), both returning refugees and newly displaced in 2003–06, a dramatic spike in 2006–09, and another wave in 2014–15 as a result of Islamic State of Iraq and Syria (ISIS) activity and increasing sectarian violence.[16] From 2006 on, when it was recognized that Iraqi refugees constituted a crisis, it has been difficult to get a handle on the number of refugees, their needs, and even assistance provided by UNHCR or others. Registering refugees was problematic from the beginning, with many refugees reluctant to register for fear it would lead to involuntary repatriation.[17] Host governments of Syria and Jordan had a vested interest in inflating the number of refugees, and UNHCR was reluctant to challenge those claims (a phenomenon seen today in Jordanian and Turkish estimates of Syrian refugee numbers). Camps for Iraqi refugees were not established in any of the host countries, but rather the refugees rented accommodations, moved in with relatives, or eked out an existence on the margins of large cities—and became largely invisible. Moreover, given the lack of refugee status in host countries in the region, the legal status of Iraqi refugees was uncertain as most were considered guests, tourists, visitors, or undocumented migrants.

The Iraqi exodus of well over a million refugees in the mid-2000s challenged the host governments, but once the Syrian exodus began in 2011, Iraqi refugees in the region became even more invisible.[18] For example, a November 2015 review of UNHCR's Iraq webpage found that the latest maps of Iraqi refugees dated back to 2008 and that most of the analysis of Iraqi refugees ended by 2010.[19]

Statistics on Iraqi refugees reveal a number of inconsistencies. Most strikingly, the number of Iraqi refugees declined from a high of 2,336,938 in 2007 to 444,471 in 2013 (the latest year for which comparable data are available.) Where did almost 2 million Iraqi refugees go? According to UNHCR figures, there were 316,075 returnees between 2006 and 2013.[20] Another 85,000 Iraqi refugees were resettled in the United States.[21] But that still leaves 1.4 million Iraqi refugees from 2006 who were neither registered in host countries in 2013 nor counted in the return or resettlement statistics. This may indicate that the 2006 figures were wildly overestimated and that the registration systems were terribly flawed. Or it may also indicate that Iraqi refugees have been able to find other solutions. It may be, for example, that some Iraqis included in the statistics for earlier years as living in the region made their way to European countries to seek asylum or join the ranks of irregular migrants.

Dawn Chatty and Nisrine Mansour argue that Iraqi refugees don't fit the Western understanding of the refugee regime because their migration is circular—Iraqi refugees return to Iraq to check on family members, pick up pension checks, etc. They characterize this mobility as the "result of a strategy to manage life risks by dispersal of family members along pre-established social networks whenever possible."[22] Many, perhaps most, of the Iraqi refugees arrived in Jordan,

Lebanon, Syria, and Egypt with some resources. But as their savings diminished and their circular movements became more precarious, their situations became more difficult.

Local integration of Iraqi refugees is rejected by all the host governments—already burned by the Palestinians—which have created various restrictions on residency, registration, and work authorization. The governments of both Jordan and Syria have claimed that the economic burden of Iraqi refugees has been very high (Syria—$1.5 billion, Jordan—$1 billion in 2008) and around 2010 began to restrict the entrance of Iraqi refugees. And yet, while integration is not possible, local "accommodation" is taking place where Iraqis are blending in with their host communities (including through intermarriage with locals) and few are deported. Interestingly, there have been virtually no cases of political violence by Iraqi refugees in any of the host countries in the region.[23]

The case of Iraqi displacement offers some clues as to what might happen in the case of the far larger outflows of Syrian refugees and some insights into the policies and attitudes of host governments. While host governments seem determined not to take any measures that will result in the permanent settlement of Syrians on their territories, positive lessons can be drawn from the experiences of both Palestinian and Iraqi refugees in the region.

Refugees who are not living in camps often find their own solutions through local accommodation when local integration is not an option, when return is impossible, or when resettlement can benefit only a small percentage of the total caseload.

THE ROOTS OF THE SYRIAN DISPLACEMENT CRISIS

While the roots of the Syrian conflict are complex and long term (and have been analyzed extensively elsewhere), the present round of violence dates back to March 2011 when Syrian protesters in the southern city of Deraa took to the streets to protest the arrest and torture of children who had painted antigovernment graffiti in public spaces. The protests did not call for the overthrow of President Bashar al-Assad but rather reflected a range of grievances.[24] Security forces responded brutally, killing some civilian protesters, and as a result, the protests spread to other cities. By June 2011 over 500 people had been killed and thousands of Syrian residents had fled into Turkey, marking the beginning of large-scale refugee movements.[25]

Former UN secretary general Kofi Annan was appointed as a Joint UN-Arab League Special Representative for Syria to negotiate an end to the conflict, but left after six months as negotiations appeared more elusive than ever. He was followed by veteran diplomat Lakhdar Brahimi, who also left in 2014 after the failure of two rounds of peace talks in Geneva between the Syrian government and opposition. The current special envoy is Steffan da Mistura, although few expect that he will be able to bring the parties to the table. At the time of this writing, the military situation on the ground continues to displace more people. The latest round of negotiations held in Vienna by the International Syrian Support Group in November 2015 and the adoption of the UN

Note that this section draws on earlier analysis by Elizabeth Ferris, Kemal Kirişci, and Salman Shaikh, "Syrian Crisis: Massive Displacement, Dire Needs and a Shortage of Solutions," Foreign Policy at Brookings, September 18, 2013.

Security Council Resolution 2254 in December, supporting efforts to seek a political solution to the conflict in Syria, are welcome developments. However, expectations of concrete progress are still not high. As International Crisis Group reported in 2013, the opposition is nearly impossible to eliminate and "the large underclass that is its core constituency has suffered such extreme regime violence that it can be expected to fight till the end."[26] This analysis is even more valid today. Discussions about a continued role for Assad in any negotiated settlement are enormously divisive. On the one hand there are fears that if Assad were to go, ISIS would fill the vacuum. On the other hand, the sheer level of violence perpetrated by the regime against the civilian population makes it difficult to see either the reintegration of refugees or long-term stability with continued rule by the regime.

A UN commission of inquiry has found that both the regime and rebels are guilty of war crimes.[27] Deadly military assaults by the government have included dropping barrel bombs on cities such as Aleppo, laying siege to rebel-held areas, and almost certainly carrying out chemical weapons attacks. A wide array of rebel groups is fighting both the regime and each other, ranging from the Western-backed Free Syrian Army to Islamist groups such as the al-Nusra Front and ISIS. At the time of writing, the Syrian government still controlled much of the country, including Damascus and the coast, but was believed to be losing its grip on the cities of Aleppo and Deraa. The Kurds control several areas of the north and north-east, while ISIS controls a large part of eastern Syria and has declared a "caliphate," which also takes in a large part of Iraq. Other opposition forces hold substantial territory around Aleppo and in the south near the Golan Heights.

Adding to the complexity of the conflict, Syria has become a key battleground for regional proxy wars. As the International Crisis Group wrote in 2013:

> The war is metastasizing in ways that draw in regional and other international actors, erase boundaries and give rise to a single, transnational arc of crisis. The opposition increasingly resembles a Sunni coalition in which a radicalized Sunni street, Islamist networks, the Syrian Muslim Brotherhood, Gulf states and Turkey take leading roles. The pro-regime camp encompassing Iran, Hezbollah, Iraq and Iraqi Shiite militants, likewise appears to be a quasi-confessional alliance.[28]

Russia, Iran, and the Lebanese militant group Hezbollah have long provided military assistance to the regime, with Russia deploying military force in direct support of the government since September 2015. On the other side, opposition forces have benefited from military and political support from countries such as Qatar, Saudi Arabia, and Turkey, in addition to "non-lethal" assistance from the United States, Britain, and other Western powers. These divisions have also played out in the diplomatic arena, with Russia and China blocking UN Security Council resolutions to impose sanctions on the Syrian regime. A round of peace talks between the Syrian government and opposition groups in Geneva collapsed in January 2014 with no agreement. There have been a handful of diplomatic breakthroughs with the Russia-backed deal for Syria to relinquish its chemical weapons arsenal, UN Security Council resolutions on cross-border aid, and more recently discussions in Vienna. However, the total lack of diplomatic consensus on how to end the conflict means that the proxy war is grinding on into its sixth year—with weapons continuing to flow to both sides from their respective backers.

The conflict has been transformed from a rebellion against an oppressive regime into a sectarian civil war. The opposition has fragmented into various Islamist networks and radical groups, such as al-Nusra and ISIS. Foreign governments and other interests are funding the war and sending fighters into Syria. An estimated 27,000 to 31,000 foreign fighters are now in Syria, and the conflict bears the hallmarks of a full-on proxy war.[29] For some, the conflict seems increasingly intended to destroy Syria as a nation-state and as a country that, while ruled by an authoritarian regime, once enjoyed reasonable prosperity, decent public services, and respect for minorities.

The following section provides a short overview of how religious minorities—Alawites, Christians, and Druze—have fared in the conflict. This theme will be picked up again in the analysis of both cross-border and internal displacement, in chapters 2 and 3, respectively.

Minorities in Syria

Arab Sunni Muslims comprise about 65 percent of the Syrian population.[30] The rest are primarily Christians, Alawites, Druze, and Ismailis, although estimates vary as the Syrian government deliberately does not keep official statistics on religious groups.[31] The (Sunni Muslim) Kurds are the largest ethnic minority. Syria has been one of the most religiously diverse countries in the Middle East, and the increasingly sectarian tone of the civil war, combined with military gains by ISIS and al-Nusra, sparked growing fears for the fate of Syria's minorities. Indeed, some in the region suggest that the sectarian nature of displacement and the particular effects on minorities are reshaping the demography of the Middle East and may end up marking the end of the nation-state in the region.[32] As will be seen in the next two chapters, displacement is both the manifestation and perhaps the cause of these changes. The Independent International Commission of Inquiry on the Syrian Arab Republic noted: "All of the Syrian Arab Republic's religious and ethnic communities are suffering as a result of the conflict. Some communities have been specifically targeted . . . in other instances, the motivations for attacks are more complex, resulting from perpetrators conflating a community's ethnic and/or religious backgrounds and its perceived political loyalties. Where ethnic or religious groups are believed to be supporters of an opposing warring faction, the entire community has been the subject of discrimination and, in some instances, violent attack."[33]

Alawites, adherents of a branch of Shia Islam, are estimated to make up 10–12 percent of Syria's population. They are considered by some to be among the most socially liberal and secular segments of Syrian society and are central to support of the Assad regime. About 75 percent of all Syrian Alawites live in the coastal Latakia region. Syrian president Bashar al-Assad hails from the Alawite minority, and his regime has traditionally commanded support from the Christian, Druze, and Ismaili minorities. While many individuals in those communities may have been critical of the regime, they tended to regard the secular Alawite government as a better alternative to possible Islamist rule. The regime also maintained power by forming an alliance with Sunni business elites and portraying itself as a bulwark against extremism to moderate Sunnis, some of whom continued to support the regime well into the uprising. While many Sunnis, especially in Damascus and Aleppo, prized stability or benefited economically from the regime, the uprising was largely driven by lower- and middle-class Sunnis from peripheral areas, who were neglected by the regime's economic liberalization policies amid a major drought.[34] While Assad's brutal response to the uprising has caused him to lose favor with Sunnis and minorities alike, the regime would not have lasted this long without a wide support base. The regime's efforts to paint the opposition as Islamic extremists (even before such groups did actually emerge) have helped to maintain the support of minority communities. At the same time, the Syrian opposition has been criticized for failing to offer an inclusive vision that guarantees the safety of minorities.[35]

While much of the Syrian army was Sunni, Alawites occupied key positions and played a major role in the violent crackdown on peaceful protesters and armed rebels. They have also made up the majority of the *shabbiha*—pro-government armed gangs accused of beating and killing protesters and carrying out atrocities such as the 2012 Houla massacre.[36] With army casualties mounting in Alawite heartlands such as Tartus, there are reports that some are no longer willing to fight for the regime in far-flung areas of Syria.[37] There is also speculation that the regime and the Alawite community will eventually withdraw to their coastal enclave and set up their own mini-state, as happened under the French mandate following World War I.

Analysts have observed mounting sectarian rhetoric against Alawites—which, combined with news of military gains by ISIS and other extremist rebel groups, have sparked fears of a genocide. While there is also serious concern about the fate of Christians and Druze, Alawites will clearly be the most vulnerable in the event of a regime collapse. In an interview with Al Jazeera, the leader of al-Nusra, Abu Mohammed al-Golani, inferred that Alawites must not only abandon Assad but convert if they don't wish to be killed.[38] (Christians would pay a special tax.) One analyst has warned of the potential for mass flight of Alawites, as well as other minorities, if the regime loses its hold on its coastal heartland.[39] As they would likely flee to unstable, over-strained Lebanon, there is dangerous potential for revenge attacks against them by other refugees as well as local communities.

Christians made up about 10 percent of Syria's population, with the largest denominations being the Greek Orthodox and Greek Catholic church.[40] Before the conflict, Syrian Christians, including Armenians, were spread throughout the country, with sizeable populations in Damascus, Homs (including surrounding areas), and Latakia. The Christian-majority villages of Saydnaya and Maaloula and the monastery of Mar Musa are outside Damascus and were popular tourist sites. Christians were perceived as supporting the regime and enjoyed a relatively high level of religious freedom. Christians have also figured among Syria's business and cultural elite and held high positions in the government and security forces. One of the leading figures of the Damascus Spring opposition movement in the early 2000s was a Christian intellectual, Michel Kilo. Ironically, one of the founders of Ba'athism, the political ideology on which the current regime rests, Michel Aflaq, was also Christian.

With violent sectarianism expected to worsen in Syria, Christians along with Alawites are considered the most vulnerable minorities.[41] Initially, some Christians in Homs and other parts of Syria had taken part in peaceful demonstrations calling for reforms, but they became increasingly alarmed due to the growing radicalization of the opposition and reports of sectarian revenge.[42] Those who were able made plans to leave Syria for Lebanon and beyond. While some Christians have tried to avoid being drawn into the conflict, others signed up with pro-government militias.[43] By 2012 sectarian slogans such as "Christians to Beirut, Alawites to the grave" were shouted at antigovernment protests although some questioned the motivation of such demonstrators.[44]

Fears of sectarian violence at the hands of rebels, if originally exaggerated by the regime, soon turned to reality. In 2014 Melkite Greek Catholic patriarch Gregorios III Laham said that more than 1,000 Christians had been killed, entire villages emptied, and dozens of churches damaged or destroyed.[45] In September 2013 the ancient Christian town of Maaloula came under attack by rebel forces led by the al-Nusra Front.[46] A number of senior Christian clerics have been kidnapped, including the heads of the Greek Orthodox and Syrian Orthodox churches in Aleppo.[47] Human Rights Watch has documented deadly indiscriminate rocket, mortar, and car bomb attacks by rebels on civilians in government-held areas, including the Christian areas of Qassa, Bab Touma, and Bab Sharqi.[48] Schools and hospitals were among the buildings hit.[49]

The fortunes of Christians worsened with the expansion of ISIS control in eastern Syria, where they have been ordered to convert to Islam, pay a special tax, or face death. As Islamic State militants advanced on Hassakeh province in February 2015, some 1,000 families fled their homes and up to 285 people were kidnapped.[50] Mounting fears over the fate of Syrian Christians in rebel-held areas have led to high-profile efforts to evacuate them.

The Druze follow a monotheistic, secretive religion drawn on Ismailism, the second largest branch of Shia Islam.[51] Their faith also incorporates elements of Christianity and Judaism and is denounced as heretical by al-Qaeda and ISIS. Druze minorities also exist in neighboring Lebanon and Israel.[52] In Syria, they are mainly concentrated in Sweida province, in Syria's south, where they make up almost 90 percent of the population.[53] They are perceived to be supportive of the regime and traditionally have high participation rates in the Ba'ath Party.[54] Druze have also fought in the Syrian army and pro-government militias, but the Druze-dominated Sweida province had remained relatively calm until recently. During summer 2015, there were fears of a massacre of Syria's Druze as rebels made gains south of Damascus.[55] The Druze were facing their most serious existential threat since the start of the conflict, with the southern Druze-dominated Sweida province under threat from ISIS and al-Nusra fighters, and the Druze forming their own security forces to protect themselves.[56]

By June 2015 Israel was preparing for the possibility of Syrian Druze refugees trying to cross into the Israeli-controlled Golan Heights, and the chief of staff of the Israel Defense Forces warned that Israel will act to prevent a massacre on its border.[57] With the situation of Syrian Druze looking far more precarious as the conflict entered its sixth year, some regional Druze leaders—including Lebanon's Walid Jumblatt—urged their co-religionists to throw their lot in with the opposition.[58] According to a report in the *Washington Post*, Druze leaders inside Syria called for neutrality, and one local spiritual leader, Wahid al-Balous, raised a militia of thousands of men (which is apparently independent from the regime) to defend the Druze.[59] There were also other reports of Druze men refusing to fight in the Syrian army so they could stay home and protect their communities.[60]

THE ESCALATING CONFLICT

Options for resolving the conflict are painfully scarce and seem to becoming more limited as the number of parties to the conflict proliferate. The UN Security Council has been paralyzed on the conflict, given the likelihood of Russian and Chinese vetoes on any meaningful action to put an end to the violence. As the conflict drags on, the possibilities for more sectarian violence increase. Many regime supporters—including Alawites, Christians and Druze—are terrified about their future, convinced that their fate is either to kill or be killed. Large-scale retribution if either side "wins" is likely.[61] Russian military intervention in support of the Assad regime is yet another complicating factor that makes it likely the war will continue. It also makes it even more unlikely that Western powers will seek to impose a no-fly zone or other form of intervention. The intensification of Russian, U.S., and coalition airstrikes in the aftermath of the November 2015 attacks in Paris add still more uncertainty to an already chaotic situation.

CONSEQUENCES OF CHAOS: MASS DISPLACEMENT

The escalation of the conflict over the past five years has had serious humanitarian consequences. As rebel forces seized control of towns in several parts of the country and as front lines shifted, sometimes on a daily or hourly basis, the challenge of accessing Syrian civilians in need of assistance became more difficult. Also, not only do front lines keep moving, but so do large numbers of Syrians seeking to escape the violence.

While millions of Syrians have fled their homes due to violence from the regime or the opposition, the military gains by ISIS have triggered further waves of massive displacement. Tens of thousands of civilians fled Kobane in late 2014 as Syrian Kurdish fighters and ISIS battled for control of the strategic town on the Turkish border. Media reports also suggest that many civilians fled ISIS-controlled cities such as Raqqa, the capital of the group's self-declared caliphate. In addition to living under ISIS's brutal rule, civilians in these areas also fear U.S., Russian, and Syrian government airstrikes.

Across the border in Iraq, the ISIS advance has had an even more devastating impact on the humanitarian situation. At least 3.2 million people have fled from areas that fell under ISIS's control between January 2014 and October 2015.[62] Almost half a million fled in June and July 2014 alone, as ISIS captured Iraq's second largest city, Mosul, and surrounding areas.[63] In August 2014 the world watched in horror the plight of tens of thousands of fleeing Yazidis facing starvation and dehydration on a mountain as ISIS took over the Sinjar area of northern Iraq.[64] While Iraqis of all faiths and ethnicities have been fleeing ISIS violence and extremist interpretation of Islamic law, minorities have been particularly vulnerable. Christians have been subjected to abuses such as the confiscation of their homes and forced conversion, while thousands of Yazidi women and girls were kidnapped and reportedly were subjected to domestic and sexual slavery.[65] Matters got worse, with ISIS in mid-2015 taking over Ramadi, the capital of Anbar province, causing more than a quarter of a million people to flee the area.[66] Overwhelmed with the scale of displacement and facing funding shortfalls, the United Nations warned in August 2015 that aid operations in Iraq were "hanging by a thread."[67]

While much of the media's attention has focused on the atrocities of ISIS in both Iraq and Syria, continuing violence by the Assad regime—particularly the 33,000 aerial bombardments carried out since the conflict began up through the summer of 2015—has been the main driver of displacement of Syrians.[68] Persistent Russian aerial bombardments made matters even worse, aggravating the displacement and accompanying humanitarian crisis.[69]

Displacement within and from Syria has been massive, dynamic, and rapid. As in other conflicts, displacement occurs for a number of reasons. Indiscriminate attacks against civilians have led many to flee the dangers of being caught in the crossfire or being deliberately targeted by armed forces. Many refugees in neighboring countries report that they fled their homes because of attacks, bombardments, or fear of being the target of military action. But there are also indications of targeted human rights violations and particularly fears about the growing sectarian nature of the conflict. The UN Commission of Inquiry found that fear of sexual violence has been a trigger for displacement, stating that "fear of rape is a driving motivation for families fleeing the violence."[70] The commission concluded that these instances of forced displacement, together with indiscriminate bombardment of civilian locations, constituted a crime against humanity and a war crime.[71]

There are also fears that displacement is being used as a tool of sectarian cleansing. Writing in November 2011, the International Crisis Group reported that "communal instincts and, in certain instances, genuine threats, are inducing citizens to resettle in like-minded areas, producing a worrying pattern of sectarian segregation."[72] As in Bosnia and Iraq, displacement is not only an unintended byproduct of conflict but also a deliberate strategy.

People are displaced not only because of direct attacks and violence but also because they can no longer survive in their communities because of the effects of the war. When people lose their jobs and cannot access basic services, they move to areas where they hope they will be able to survive, often first within the country and then later across a border into a neighboring country.

It is difficult to overestimate the impact of the war on normal life in Syria. The destruction of utilities and essential infrastructure, and the unraveling of public services such as waste disposal, electricity, fuel, education, and medical care have disrupted the functioning of life on all levels. In March 2015 the United Nations Development Program reported that 80 percent of Syrians inside the country were living in poverty, life expectancy has plunged by 20 years, and the economy had lost $200 billion since the conflict began. It estimated that 3 million Syrians had lost their jobs during the conflict, with unemployment surging from 14.9 percent in 2011 to 57.7 percent at the end of 2014. Over 50 percent of children were not attending school in 2014.[73] Indeed, the lack of opportunities for children to continue their education seems to be a driving force of displacement.

GENDER AND SYRIAN DISPLACEMENT

Civilian men make up the largest group of victims, the UN Commission of Inquiry said in its August 2015 report. "Civilian men perceived to be of fighting age have been targeted by warring parties during ground attacks. They are also the primary civilian victims of enforced disappearance, torture and unlawful killing."[74] Men are arbitrarily arrested by the government and detained because of their own actions or to pressure family members wanted by the authorities. There is a countrywide pattern in which mainly adult male civilians have been seized by government forces and then disappeared. The government's expanding conscription policies have become a major cause of displacement, both internally and cross-border.[75] The UN Commission added that "multiple accounts have been documented of women leaving their husbands behind in opposition-held areas to accompany their pre-adolescent sons through the checkpoints and out of the area before they reach an age where they are likely to be stopped by Government forces."[76] ISIS also has forcibly recruited men and boys and imposed restrictions on those living in areas under their control, including dress codes and prohibitions against being in the company of women to whom they are not related.[77]

Women and girls have been targeted on the basis of their gender by both government and opposition forces. "For the belligerents, the very act of detaining a woman, with all the risks to her person that this implies, appears designed to humiliate not only the woman, but also—and arguably, primarily—her male relatives," the UN Commission reported. "Women have suffered rape and other forms of sexual violence by government personnel while held in detention facilities." Because women can move more freely than men in government-controlled areas, they are at increased risk of physical and sexual assault. When their male family members are detained or disappear, women are often left with no means of supporting themselves. Without confirmation of deaths of husbands or fathers, they are in legal limbo, unable to inherit or sell property or to remarry. As mentioned above, violence against women has increased dramatically as a result of ISIS's growing control of territory and population. In ISIS areas, women and girls over the age of ten may not appear publicly without being entirely covered and may not travel without a close male relative. For women whose husbands have died, have fled, or are at the battlefront, this means that they cannot leave their homes for any reason without risking punishment.[78]

Given the escalating levels of violence inside Syria, it is perhaps not surprising that so many Syrians have fled their communities. The number of registered refugees in neighboring countries increased from 8,000 in 2011 to almost 500,000 only a year later, and was well over four million in late 2015 (see figure 1-2). Close to 500,000 Syrians entered Europe in 2015 by sea, making up the largest segment of the more than 1 million who sought safety in Europe during the year. Meanwhile the number of people displaced inside Syria has continued to rise, with estimates in late 2015 reaching 6.5 million.[79]

STAGGERING AMOUNTS—BUT STILL NOT ENOUGH FUNDING

As the Syrian crisis is in its fifth year, it is getting harder to mobilize the necessary minimum humanitarian assistance. If there is a silver lining to the movement of Syrians to Europe in August–September 2015, it is that donor countries are stepping up their contributions—perhaps recognizing the link between inadequate support to refugees in the region and the hundreds of thousands of Syrians now traveling to European borders. The European Union has already made promises to increase substantially its financial support for neighboring host countries.

Table 1-1 summarizes the international response to UN appeals for Syria and the region. These figures show

- Steadily increasing appeals for international assistance, with the request in 2015 almost ten times the amount requested in 2012;

FIGURE 1-2. *Number of Syrian Refugees, 2011–15*

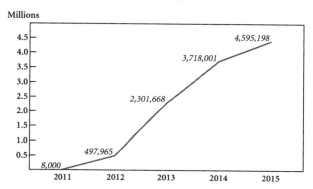

Source: United Nations High Commissioner for Refugees, "Syria Regional Refugee Response."

■ More funds requested for supporting refugees than affected civilians inside Syria although the numbers of the latter are far higher. This is at least partly the consequence of difficulties in accessing populations in need in Syria; and

■ A disproportionate (although still seriously insufficient) amount of appeals for the Syrian crisis rather than for other crises in the world.

Almost half of the worldwide appeal for humanitarian funding was requested for Syria. At the end of 2014 the UN appealed for $16.4 billion to assist 57 million people in 22 countries.[80] To put it another way, the $4.5 billion appeal for 4 million Syrian refugees works out to about $1,125 per refugee. In comparison, the appeal for $16.4 billion for the global total of 57 million people (which includes the Syrian refugees) comes to about $290 per person.

These funding disparities raise questions, not just for

TABLE 1-1. *Syria and Regional Response Funding, 2012–15*

Year	Appeal[a]	Amount of appeal (USD)[b]	Funds received	% of appeal received
2012	Syria Regional Refugee Response Plan (RRP)	488 million	374 million	77
2012	Syrian Humanitarian Assistance Response Plan (SHARP)	348 million—71% of refugee appeal	216 million	62
2013	Syria Regional Refugee Response Plan (RRP)	3 billion	2.2 billion	73
2013	Syrian Humanitarian Assistance Response Plan (SHARP)	1.4 billion—47% of refugee appeal	956 million	68
2014	Syria Regional Refugee Response Plan (RRP)	3.7 billion	2.4 billion	63
2014	Syrian Humanitarian Assistance Response Plan (SHARP)	2.3 billion—62% of refugee appeal	1.1 billion	49
2015	Syria Regional Refugee and Resilience Plan (3RP)	4.5 billion	2.68 billion	59
2015	Syria Strategic Response Plan (SRP)	2.9 billion—65% of refugee appeal	1.25 billion	43

Source: United Nations, Office for the Coordination of Humanitarian Affairs (OCHA), Financial Tracking Service, "Syrian Arab Republic—Funding Received," November 9, 2015 (https://fts.unocha.org/pageloader.aspx?page=emerg-emergencyCountryDetails&cc=syr).

a. SHARP (followed by the SRP in 2015) refers to assistance inside Syria, while the Regional Refugee Response Plan (3RP in 2015) targets refugees in neighboring countries.

b. Percentage shows the difference between appeals for refugees and for assistance inside Syria, including for IDPs.

Syrian refugees in the region and for those displaced by the conflict inside Syria, but for the future of the international humanitarian system—a theme to which we will return in the final chapter of this study.

What does this mean for the regional response to Syrian refugees? In comparison with other major crises, the Syrian response has been well-funded, although the UN appeals have never been fully funded. If international assistance decreases, this will increase the pressure on host governments—which are already doing everything they can to reduce the number of Syrian arrivals, discourage them from living lives of dignity and self-reliance, and encourage them to return to Syria. One of the rarely discussed realities is that international aid supports protection of the human rights of refugees and the internally displaced. Host governments allow refugees to stay partly in exchange for international financial support. The borders of all of Syria's neighbors are now effectively closed, with the exception of Turkey, although specific border crossings also open and close depending on the conflict.

We turn now to an examination of the Syrian refugee phenomenon—and the impact of the refugees on the governments and societies which host them.

CHAPTER 2

Syrian Refugees: Challenges to Host Countries and the International Community

The scale of refugee movements from Syria has been both rapid and massive. A full year after the first disturbances in Syria, the number of registered Syrian refugees in the neighboring countries was just over 26,000.[1] Nearly four years later, as of end-December 2015, this total was just under 4.6 million.[2] None of the host governments expected the displacement either to reach such a scale or to last this long.

The initial displacement occurred against the optimistic background of the early days of the Arab Spring and thus under the assumption that any displacement caused by popular uprisings in Syria would be of a very temporary nature. Many in the region (and outside the region as well) initially believed the Syrian regime would be replaced by a reformist one, mirroring the transition that had just taken place in Tunisia and Egypt. Instead, the situation in Syria escalated into a civil war. Indiscriminate government attacks on and repression of civilians forced more and more people to become either internally displaced or flee into neighboring countries. Since the summer of 2014, additional displacement has resulted from the brutal treatment of civilians by the Islamic State in Iraq and Syria (ISIS) and from fighting between ISIS and other opposition groups. The Russian intervention in the Syrian civil war in support of the Syrian government since September 2015 has led to further displacement and to prospects that the situation could get even worse.

The registered refugee populations in Lebanon and Jordan have by and large remained stable at around 630,000 since early 2014 in Jordan and around 1.1 million since late 2014 in Lebanon, the results of hardening border policies in both countries (see figure 2-1).[3] In the case of Turkey, the number of refugees has continued to increase, reaching 2.5 million as of the end of December 2015.[4] The escalation of violence in and around Aleppo, partly resulting from Russian intervention but also engendered by pro-regime factions, is expected to precipitate the displacement of up to another 3 million people toward Turkey.[5] In the meantime,

FIGURE 2-1. *Refugee Population, by Country, 2011–15*

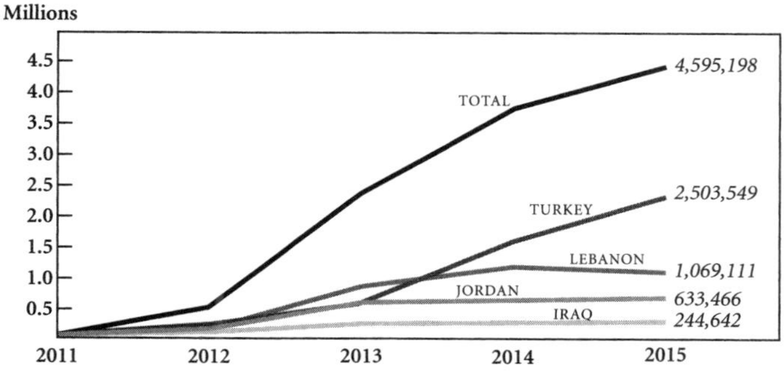

Source: United Nations High Commissioner of Refugees, Syrian Regional Refugee Response.

the actual number of registered Syrian refugees in Turkey increased by almost half a million between early October and late December—and that in spite of the movement of Syrians leaving Turkey for Europe.[6] Approximately 245,000 and 117,000 registered Syrian refugees are in Iraq and Egypt, respectively, together with another estimated 28,000 refugees in North African countries. The majority of the refugees live outside camps in these five host countries. Most of the refugees are Sunni, but minorities such as Armenians, Assyrians, Kurds, Roma, and Yazidis have also joined their ranks.

As noted in the previous chapter, with the exception of Turkey the other host countries are not signatories of the 1951 Geneva Convention on the Status of Refugees. This means that Syrian refugees do not have the possibility of receiving a full-fledged refugee status, and instead are considered "guests"—an ill-defined status offering no legal protection. In effect, the situation is not very different in Turkey, as Turkey maintains a "geographical limitation" that limits the application of the Geneva Convention to those asylum-seekers who have become refugees as a result of "events occurring in Europe."[7] This means that Turkey neither grants refugee status to Syrians nor allows them the possibility of remaining in the country for the long term. Resettlement and voluntary repatriation are seen as the only durable solutions. Instead of being recognized as refugees with rights, Syrians are granted "temporary protection" in Turkey.

The role and status of the United Nations High Commissioner for Refugees (UNHCR) vary across these host countries. UNHCR has been involved in the registration of refugees—a critical process in terms of ensuring protection and access to basic services, including education, health, food, and social support. In Jordan and Lebanon, UNHCR has also been the lead international agency in ensuring basic humanitarian assistance for the refugees and managing the camps. All of these countries have extended generous support to the refugees, but none has allowed the refugees to work legally, dramatically limiting their ability to gain access to legal livelihoods and improve their living conditions.

In the meantime, there is now a general consensus that many, possibly most, Syrian refugees will remain in neighboring countries for the foreseeable future. This raises a host of questions, especially for Jordan, Lebanon, and Turkey—the three countries that have received 90 percent of the refugees registered in Syria's neighborhood. What has been the economic, social, and political impact on these three countries of the refugee crisis? How has the international response evolved? How can the cooperation between these three countries and the international community in addressing the needs of refugees be improved? Are there lessons to be learned? These questions are the focus of this chapter.

THE GROWING REFUGEE CRISIS

In addition to the significant increase in numbers, there are three striking differences between the refugee situation today and that of only a few years ago. Firstly, the ethnic and religious background of the refugees has become much more diverse, especially in the case of Turkey. Originally, the refugees were overwhelmingly Arab Sunni Syrians with a smaller number of Turcomans and Alawites. Today, they have been joined by Kurds from northern Syria as well as Yazidis and Christians from Iraq. Some 40,000 to 50,000 Iraqis fled to Turkey following the capture of Mosul and its environs by ISIS in June 2014; later, the Peshmergha forces of the Kurdish regional government as well as the U.S. airstrikes were able to push back against the ISIS onslaught. By the time the situation stabilized, however, the number had increased to about 240,000–250,000.[8] The Turkish government and various municipalities constructed camps to house some of the refugees, while most settled into villages and towns in southeastern Turkey inhabited by their coreligionists or ethnic brethren. Another mass exodus occurred in October 2014, when around 170,000 Syrians, most of them Kurds, fled the fighting between the Democratic Union Party (PYD, from the Kurdish, Partiya Yekîtiya Demokrat) and ISIS in Kobane. Some of these refugees have since returned, although some still live in one large government camp and smaller municipal camps, while others remain dispersed throughout Turkey's Suruç region, across the border from Kobane.

In June 2015 clashes erupted between ISIS and the PYD forces along with their Syrian Arab allies—this time for the control of the Syrian border town of Tel Abyad. About 25,000 Arabs, Kurds, and Turcomans fled into Turkey under chaotic circumstances. Most of the refugees who escaped into Lebanon and Jordan were Sunni Arabs from the central and southern parts of Syria; some were Christians. In the fall of 2015 Russian military intervention aggravated the situation. Then in November 2015, just days before the downing of a Russian fighter plane by Turkey, there were reports of Turcomans being displaced to the Turkish-Syrian border where a makeshift camp was set up for them.[9] Subsequent Russian operations in the area became even more forceful, undermining humanitarian assistance efforts and causing additional displacement.[10] The very real possibility of increased confrontations between various Syrian opposition groups and ISIS, as well as Russia, in areas close to Turkey risks aggravating the displacement crisis. One Turkish report estimated that another "3 to 5 million Syrians are expected to leave their country."[11]

Secondly, the political response of countries receiving Syrian refugees has also dramatically changed, particularly for Jordan and Turkey. The governments there received the first waves of refugees with open arms. This was partly driven by the fact that the refugee numbers initially were limited, and both governments believed the regime in Damascus would soon collapse and the refugees could return home quickly. They thus instituted an "open door policy" and began to set up camps for the refugees. Jordan invited UNHCR to manage the camps and co-register the refugees. In Turkey, camps were set up and run by the Disaster and Emergency Management Agency, while the government formally extended temporary protection to the refugees in October 2011, stating that it would manage the situation without international assistance.[12]

However, much sooner than expected, both Ankara's and Amman's hopes that the refugees would be able to return to a reformed Syria were dashed.[13] Instead, Turkey became increasingly embroiled in efforts to overthrow the Assad regime through active support for the opposition, including radical Islamic groups.[14] Furthermore, as the cost of maintaining Syrian refugees rapidly increased, Turkey sought greater international support and persistently called for the establishment of a "safe haven" for refugees inside Syria, though with little success on either count.[15] Jordan, unlike Turkey, did not completely rupture its relations with the Syrian regime and eventually succeeded in creating a kind of informal safe zone that enabled some refugees to return to southern Syria. Jordan was also able both to mobilize more international assistance for refugees and to limit the flow of refugees into its territory. Although the Jordanian government continues to identify its policy as "open doors," human rights and international nongovernmental organization officials note that it is not really the case in practice.[16] Turkey's track record in this regard has also been questioned, with cases of *refoulement* (expelling refugees back into dangerous situations), forced returns, and other violations of the government's "open door" policy being frequently reported.[17] These practices have reportedly increased since the deal reached between the European Union and Turkey in November to stem the flow of Syrian refugees (discussed further below).[18]

The case of Lebanon is somewhat different. The long-standing governmental deadlock engendered by the failure to elect a new president and sensitivity over delicate sectarian balances, especially between the Sunni and Shia communities in Lebanon, have shaped the government's response to the Syrian crisis. The near-paralysis of the government initially resulted in "semi-laissez faire" policy, enabling refugees to enter the country unhindered. Lebanon's previous experiences with Palestinians and the lessons drawn from the long civil war between 1975 and 1990 led the government to prohibit the establishment of refugee camps.[19] Instead, hundreds of small makeshift settlements have sprung up to house those refugees who have been unable to find better shelter. Furthermore, the fragile sectarian situation and the fact that Hezbollah, the leading Shia Lebanese political actor, has been actively supporting the regime in Syria have strained Lebanon's capacity to receive large numbers of primarily Sunni refugees. Alarmed by the reality that by early 2015 the number of Syrian refugees surpassed one-fourth of Lebanon's own population, the government put in place a visa requirement for Syrians to enter Lebanon and then stopped registering any further refugees.[20] In effect, this led to the abandonment of Lebanon's open-door policy. At the same time, the precipitous decrease in humanitarian aid, coupled with administrative measures that made the renewal of residency permits more difficult and expensive, has led some Syrians to leave Lebanon.[21] Meanwhile, those who remain behind are trapped in a vicious cycle of insecurity.[22]

The third factor is that the worsening refugee crisis has deepened the social, economic, and political problems of the host countries. The massive growth in the number of refugees outside camps and the lack of adequate assistance policies toward them have aggravated a range of social problems. Refugees experience problems of adaptation especially in urban settings (where most are living) in terms of access to shelter and basic services such as education and health care. An added problem in the case of Turkey is the language barrier that complicates the refugees' ability to cope with the challenges of day-to-day survival.

Now that the initially generous welcome has worn thin, public opinion toward refugees is becoming increasingly negative. The sight of Syrians begging in the streets is causing particular resentment among local people, especially in cities in western Turkey. There have also been reports of occasional violence between refugees and locals.[23] In turn, this reinforces a growing public perception that associates Syrian refugees with criminality. A public opinion poll conducted in Turkey in October 2014 revealed that more than 62 percent of those surveyed supported the idea that Syrian refugees were implicated in criminality and were responsible for the uptick in the number of crimes committed.[24] As early as 2013, a poll in Lebanon found that 52 percent of respondents believed Syrian refugees posed a threat to national security and stability, and more than 90 percent said the Syrian conflict had a negative impact on the Lebanese government's capacity to protect Lebanese citizens.[25] These concerns persist, and a survey in June 2015 noted that almost half of those surveyed fear for their personal safety because of the refugees.[26] Similar complaints also have been made in Jordan.[27] Yet these attitudes represent a stark contrast with local authorities' and security officials' observations in all three countries: in reality, criminality is surprisingly low, and Syrian community leaders are very effective in preventing crime and defusing tensions between refugees and locals.

The presence of large numbers of refugees, especially in urban centers, generates competition for public services with local residents. The cost of providing these services to a growing number of refugees, together with the costs of the camps in Jordan and Turkey, fuels the resentment of local communities. In the case of Turkey, this is heightened by the fact that the government continues to allocate funds from its own budget to pay for dealing with the refugees. This practice hits a particular nerve among the locals, who feel that it undermines their own access to, for instance, health services, while health personnel are occupied to an overwhelming degree with the refugees.[28] Not surprisingly, 71 percent of the Turkish public told pollsters that Syrian refugees have cost the economy dearly, and 60 percent objected to their taxes being spent on the refugees.[29] Similar observations can also be made for education, especially in Jordan and Lebanon, where both governments have opened their schools to Syrian refugee children. In Lebanon, there are now more Syrian children in public schools than Lebanese children, in part reflecting the dominance of the private educational system unaffordable for the refugees.[30] Jordan has scheduled teaching staff in double-shifts to accommodate the new students and handle overcrowded classrooms.[31] On the other hand, cost considerations and public opinion have led the Jordanian government to scale down substantially the refugees' access to public health services.

The Economic Impact of the Refugees

The urban refugees present very visible economic problems. One striking case in point is the increase in prices in general, but especially in the real estate market—which gives rise to additional complaints among local residents. Furthermore, many refugees are employed informally and often are prepared to work for lower wages than locals.[32] In Turkey, 69 percent of the public in the regions close to Syria believe that refugees are taking away their jobs.[33] A similar survey finding is also reported in Lebanon.[34] This feeling also is widely shared in Jordan. The fact that refugees neither pay taxes nor make contributions to social security expenses creates additional distortions in the economy. This situation not only makes Syrian refugees vulnerable to exploitation but also generates resentment, especially from local unskilled workers looking for employment in the informal sector. The reluctance of governments to open the labor market to refugees or to support livelihoods for them appears to further aggravate the situation, especially in Jordan and Lebanon, where subsistence assistance to refugees has been substantially curtailed.[35]

In spite of these negative consequences, the refugee crisis has also led to an increase in economic activity and added more positions for skilled laborers in host countries. The growth in the number of national and international nongovernmental organizations and specialized agencies aiding Syrian refugees has created opportunities for employment in the host countries and set the conditions for economic growth through their demand for local goods and ser-vices.[36] Regional cities such as Amman, Beirut, Gaziantep, Kilis, and others have become visible hubs of humanitar-ian activity. Furthermore, the three neighboring countries have become important suppliers of humanitarian and other goods being sent into Syria. For example, the Turkish provinces sharing a border with Syria saw their exports to Syria rise by more than 200 percent from 2011 to 2014, while the overall increase for Turkey's exports to Syria in general was only 11 percent.[37] As much as Jordan and Lebanon have seen their exports to Syria fluctuate, they have nevertheless continued to be important suppliers of fresh and processed food, household goods, and construction materials.[38] Ad-ditionally, greater economic activity has been spurred by small and larger businesses, often in the form of restaurants but also factories set up by Syrians who were able to bring their capital to Jordan, Lebanon, and Turkey. For example, according to a study by the Economic Policy Research Foun-dation of Turkey, the number of companies established in Turkey with Syrian shareholders increased to 1,256 in 2014 from just 30 such companies in 2010.[39] Including the "in-formal" Syrian business establishments increased the 2014 figure to more than 10,000.[40] One Jordanian economist remarked that refugees increased demand "by using their wages to rent apartments, buying goods and services, put-ting factories and retailers to work."[41] Similar observations can be made for Lebanon.

However, there is also a downside to this picture. Syrian refugees have become a source of cheap labor willing to work in positions that local workers are reluctant to take up. With-out legal employment, as one Turkish academic in Gazian-tep noted, the educated and middle-class Syrian refugees are reduced to cheap labor.[42] Furthermore, the failure to generate livelihoods is forcing refugee families to resort to "negative coping mechanisms." There is a serious problem of child labor across the three host countries, as children are less likely to be arrested for working illegally than are adult men and women. In Jordan and Lebanon, the case is aggravated by a desire to circumvent the risk of detention and deportation for illegal employment.[43] Similarly, families are allowing and encouraging underage girls to marry early, even submitting their daughters to polygamous marriages.[44] This presents a legal problem in Turkey, where marriage under the age of eighteen and polygamy are both prohibited by law. There are growing concerns among women and human rights advocates that the spread of this practice risks undermining the effectiveness of the law, especially at a time when a recent constitutional court ruling in Turkey has decriminalized religious weddings without civil marriage.[45] Some women who are desperate to feed their families now resort to prostitution—yet another example of the negative social impact the presence of Syrian refugees is having on host societies. A Joint Agency Briefing Paper prepared by a group of international nongovernmental organizations said this picture has become the norm for refugees, adding: "More and more refugees are being pushed to make desperate choices. Children are forced to leave school and work illegally, girls are forced into marriage before their time, and many have little option but to risk their lives on dangerous boat journeys in the hope of reaching Europe, or even to return to Syria."[46]

Political Consequences

The continued influx of large numbers of refugees has also had political consequences. As noted above, public reaction toward refugees has shifted from a generous welcome to calls for their departure. These calls, however, are not uniform and are influenced by ethnic and religious affinities. In Turkey, for example, religiously conservative Turks and Turkish citizens of Arab descent, often members of the governing Justice and Development Party constituency, have consistently supported the government's openness to receiving the bulk of the refugees, provided that they are Sunni Arabs.[47] Secular Turks, Alevis, and Kurds, by contrast, fear the prospect of welcoming large numbers of Sunni Arabs, as they may change the demographics of local society and politics.[48] Interestingly, since the influx of refugees from Kobane, Kurdish views on Syrian refugees have become more aligned with those of ruling party supporters.[49]

Yet, at the same time, the reluctance of the Turkish government to assist the Kurds in their resistance to the onslaught of ISIS in Kobane in the fall of 2014 and an initial hesitation to allow Kurdish refugees to enter Turkey deeply scarred Kurds' trust in the Turkish government. The situation continued to worsen in the run-up to the national elections in Turkey in June 2015, as the Kurdish People's Democratic Party campaigned against the government. Subsequently, tensions between the Kurds and the Turkish government were exacerbated by the deaths of more than 30 people in July 2015 in a bombing in the Turkish town of Suruç across from Kobane, followed by a similar bombing in Ankara in October that killed more than 100 people and that was orchestrated by ISIS-affiliated suicide bombers. The cycle of violence that followed these events killed hundreds of civilians, Kurdish militants, and security forces—and continues to pose a threat to the stability of Turkey. Turkey's Kurdish-populated Southeast increasingly looks like Iraq and Syria.[50] It is very difficult to understand this sudden escalation without appreciating the impact that the siege of

Kobane and the arrival of Kurdish refugees from Kobane have had on Turkish domestic politics.[51]

In Lebanon, the political impact of Syrian refugees has been a particularly acute concern. Not surprisingly, the arrival of refugees that eventually constituted a fourth of the population—in a country where demographic balances among the Sunni, Shia, and Christians have always been at the center of politics—has produced negative ramifications.[52] This has been further complicated because most refugees are Sunni and have fled Syria as a result of government attacks on their communities. One leading player in Lebanese politics, Hezbollah, is actually an overt ally of the Syrian regime, and its foot soldiers have directly fought in support of the regime and against Syrian opposition groups.[53] In turn, Syrian rebels, including radical Islamic groups, have even attacked Hezbollah positions along the Syrian-Lebanese border.[54] These developments created a very tense situation in certain parts of Lebanon such as the Bekaa Valley where many Syrian refugees have settled. Clearly, the civil war in Syria has directly affected Lebanon's domestic politics—to the extent that it has run the risk of reigniting a civil war.[55] More recently the November 2015 suicide bombings in Beirut, for which ISIS claimed responsibility, demonstrated Lebanon's vulnerability to violence in the region.[56]

Lebanon has a long and torturous relationship with Syria, which historically had difficulties in accepting Lebanon's existence as a separate and independent state. Syria was deeply involved in the Lebanese civil war, and for years afterward many people considered Lebanon to be under Syria's occupation.[57] This occupation came to an abrupt end after the 2005 assassination of Rafik Hariri, a former prime minister. Even after Syria's withdrawal, the close relationship between the two countries did not end, and many Syrians continued to live and work in Lebanon, some of whom actually became refugees *sur place* after the eruption of the Syrian conflict.[58] The refugees and Syria's particular legacy in Lebanon fuel fears of a repetition of the situation when the influx of Palestinian refugees in 1948 and subsequent developments launched the protracted journey toward the Lebanese civil war.[59]

This legacy of Palestinian refugees also plays a role in shaping Jordan's concerns regarding the impact of Syrian refugees. The arrival of more than half a million Syrian refugees evoked, in the minds of the public and the leadership, the memories of the influx of Palestinian refugees in 1948 and again in 1967. These memories include a violent uprising in 1971, when radical Palestinian groups rebelled against the Hashemite kingdom.[60] This experience left a deep imprint on Jordanian sense of national identity and national security, highlighting the importance of maintaining the delicate balance between "East Bankers" and Jordanians of Palestinian descent. More than 2 million Palestinians are still registered in the refugee camps across Jordan; the arrival and the continuing presence of more than half a million Syrian refugees therefore creates a politically sensitive situation for a country of only 6.7 million. Furthermore, somewhat like in Turkey, one's political affiliation does play a role in determining attitudes toward the Syrian refugees. Trends indicate that sympathizers of the Muslim Brotherhood in Jordan, compared with the more nationalist and secular Jordanians, are more likely to support the welcoming approach.

MANAGING THE REFUGEE INFLUX

Often overlooked is modern Turkey's long history as a country of asylum and immigration. Between the establishment of the Turkish Republic in 1923 and roughly the end of the Cold War, it received more than 1.5 million immigrants from the Balkans.[61] Turkey also served as a country of asylum for individuals fleeing the Soviet bloc during the Cold War years. There were also mass influxes of refugees from Bulgaria and Iraq in 1989 and 1991. Since then, Turkey has received numerous applications from the nationals of a wide array of Asian and African countries, and it was listed by the UNHCR as the fourth largest recipient of individual asylum-seekers in 2014.[62]

As discussed earlier, unlike Jordan and Lebanon, Turkey is a signatory to the 1951 Geneva Convention on the Status of Refugees, but it grants "full" refugee status only to asylum-seekers who have fled "events occurring in Europe."[63] Other asylum-seekers are granted the right to remain in Turkey only until their resettlement can be arranged. This practice was incorporated into the Law on Foreigners and International Protection adopted in April 2013.[64] As of May 2015 Turkey was host to 230,000 non-Syrian individual asylum-seekers, mostly Afghans, Iraqis, Iranians, and Somalis.[65]

There are certainly similarities (as mentioned above) in how each of these countries has received and managed the refugee crisis. However, as the crisis persisted, each country developed its own unique approach. Jordan worked much more closely with the international community and pushed harder for international burden sharing; but as the crisis wore on, the government cut back on the benefits for refugees, public opinion soured, and national resources became strained. Unlike Jordan, Lebanon, as a function of its paralyzed state and weak government, introduced a kind of "semi laissez faire" approach that has left refugees either to survive on their own resources or from those offered by the international community. Like its Jordanian counterpart, the Lebanese government has energetically denied refugees the possibility of legal employment and since 2014 has also introduced restrictions on new arrivals and imposed new fees and procedures for renewing residency permits. Turkey, on the other hand, followed a distinctive approach. Initially it turned away international assistance and tried to manage the crisis on its own. As Turkey's plans failed to create a safe-zone in Syria, where would-be refugees could live instead of entering Turkey, the Turkish leadership developed an uneasy relationship with the international community. This relationship oscillated between pragmatism and harsh criti-cism. In the meantime, the government continued to extend assistance, but, like Jordan and Lebanon, it, until recently, did not allow the refugees to take up jobs legally (although more and more refugees reportedly worked in the informal sector).

Initially Jordan set up the Zaatari camp, south of its border with Syria, for the refugees, with a peak popula-tion in March 2013 of more than 150,000. This camp then became Jordan's third largest city and was subsequently fol-lowed with the construction of additional camps.[66] Simul-taneously, Jordan engaged the cooperation of the UNHCR as well as other international agencies, allowing them to manage the day-to-day affairs of the camp. However, as the numbers continued to increase and the conflict in Syria es-calated, the expectation of a quick return was replaced by growing concerns about the political implications of per-manent camps. As discussed in detail above, past experi-ence with Palestinian refugees accentuated these concerns. Jordan very quickly instituted, together with UNHCR, a registration process for urban refugees and made regis-tration a requirement for access to such public services as health and education. Jordan also welcomed a long list of in-ternational agencies to help support the needs of refugees in coordination with the Ministry of Planning and the Hashemite Charity Organization.

The size of the refugee population and the protracted nature of the conflict in Syria have put dramatic strains on Jordan's financial and limited natural resources, including water.[67] The government has virulently complained about inadequate burden sharing on the part of the international community and pushed for greater funding to support the refugees. The point was made starkly by King Abdullah II during his address to the UN General Assembly in September 2015 at the height of the European refugee crisis.[68] This concern for greater economic support is not surprising. According to some, hosting refugees who make up more than 10 percent of the population in a relatively small and resource-poor country even runs the risk of transforming Jordan from a "middle income" to a "low income" country.[69] Furthermore, the mounting economic cost of hosting the refugees has created tension between the Jordanian government and international agencies, as the sides disagree over the actual number of refugees under the government's care. While the UNHCR put the number of Syrian refugees at around 630,000 in October 2015, the government insisted that the actual figure was more like 1.4 million. The government was not quite transparent about how it arrived at this figure, which appeared to include Syrians who were already in the country before the crisis erupted.[70] Furthermore, motivated by sensitivity toward public opinion, the government demanded that a greater share of international assistance be directed toward local communities. This was starkly reflected in the Jordan Resilience Plan, whose focus was primarily on programs for local communities rather than the refugees.[71]

Budgetary concerns coupled with domestic political considerations also led the government to cut off health subsidies for refugees and deny refugees access to the local labor market. These developments coincided with a drastic scaling down of support from the World Food Program, leaving an increasing number of the refugees in particularly vulnerable situations. Inability to maintain a livelihood and the utterly desperate situation that many Syrian refugees found themselves in pushed an increasing number of Syrians to return to Syria and/or to travel from Jordan on to Europe.[72] These returns were also prompted by the relative calm in southern regions of Syria that border Jordan. In October 2015 the returns to Syria were estimated to be around 140 a day.[73] However, among human rights and some international agency circles there were concerns that these returns might not have been voluntary and therefore not in line with international law.[74] This concern was aggravated by a government practice that made it increasingly difficult for Syrians to enter Jordan and benefit from what was fast becoming a "not-so-open-door policy."

Lebanon, largely because of the Palestinian experience, decided right from the beginning not to set up refugee camps. Instead, refugees were initially sheltered in available housing and accommodation centers but subsequently were left to fend for themselves. As a result, a large proportion of the more than 1.1 million refugees had to build their own makeshift shelters (referred to as "informal tented settlements") while some managed to rent accommodations, usually of very poor quality. One of the few measures the Lebanese government introduced, beyond following strictly their registration, was to allow Syrian refugee children access to schools. Actually, more than half of the students regis-

tered in Lebanese schools as of mid-2015 were Syrian children.[75] Refugees had to rely on their own means for meeting
their health needs or to seek access to services provided by
international agencies and their nongovernmental partners
responsible for implementation. The government worked
closely with the World Food Program to make a food cash
program available for refugees. However, lack of funds led
to a severe curtailment of the program in 2015. This was aggravated by the government's longstanding decision not to
allow refugees to work legally. In an effort to maintain their
livelihoods, many resorted to negative coping mechanisms
such as child labor and prostitution—increasing the pressure on refugees to return to Syria or to leave Lebanon for
other destinations.[76]

To Europe via Turkey

The decision to end Lebanon's "open door" policy in late
2014 and the introduction of major and costly administrative measures increasingly complicated the possibility for
Syrian refugees to stay in Lebanon.[77] National security considerations and especially the role of Hezbollah in Lebanon's
executive circles and its support for the Assad regime suggested that this trend was not likely to change in the near
future. It was therefore not surprising that some refugees felt
obliged to return to the precarious circumstances prevailing
in Syria, and those who could not afford to take such risks
attempted to make it to Europe.

Turkey began to receive its first refugees from Syria as
early as April 2011, and like Jordan and Lebanon adopted an
"open door" policy. In the initial stages of the crisis, refugees
were mostly housed in schools, sports halls, unused ware-

houses, and factories. As the numbers continued to increase, the Disaster and Emergency Management Agency was given the task of constructing purpose-built camps for refugees while the government formally extended "temporary protection" to Syrian refugees in October 2011.[78] In less than two years more than twenty camps had been set up, housing about 200,000 refugees. Soon it became evident that the agency could not go on constructing camps, as more and more refugees arrived and preferred to live in urban settings. The government made provisional arrangements to ensure access to health services, but it was not until October 2014 that the government adopted what it called a Temporary Protection Circular to define temporary protection, instituted registration of the refugees, and established coordination between different agencies to provide better services for urban refugees.[79] The disaster agency remained responsible for establishing and running refugee camps as well as ensuring emergency assistance for new arrivals, while the Directorate General for Migration Management took over the task of registration and overall coordination. As of late December 2015 almost 2.5 million refugees were registered, with more than a quarter of a million of them living in twenty-five refugee camps, including five camps set up specifically to house Christians, Kurds, and Yazidis. Another 200,000 to 250,000 refugees had failed to register for a variety of reasons, and some commentators believe that many of the Syrian refugees that fled to Europe were among them.[80]

Managing the presence of more than 2.5 million refugees has not been an easy task—even for a country with significant administrative and economic capacity. This was complicated by an initial reluctance by the government to seek international assistance. Turkey chose not to be included in the first Syrian Regional Response Plan of the UN and preferred not to cooperate with the UNHCR beyond ensuring supplies of tents for camps and overseeing voluntary return. However, as the burden of refugees dramatically increased, the Turkish government started to coordinate more with international agencies such as the International Organization on Migration, UNHCR, UNICEF, the World Food Program, and the World Health Organization.[81] After initial resistance by the government, a range of international non-governmental organizations (NGOs) also established themselves in Turkey. They worked with a growing number of Turkish and Syrian NGOs to respond to the needs of urban refugees by supporting activities that ranged from teaching language courses, including Turkish, to running courses to help women acquire vocational skills and psycho-social support programs.[82] Unlike Lebanon and Jordan, Turkey never put into place a comprehensive food cash support program for urban refugees beyond modest and limited programs offered by some NGOs.[83]

As much as Turkey's hosting of Syrian refugees received wide-ranging praise (including from the authors), Turkey's management of the presence of Syrian refugees has not been without difficulties.[84] One immediate problem had to do with access to the services promised under the Temporary Protection Circular. Amnesty International and others reported that Syrian refugees on occasion were denied entry into Turkey, especially in the case of Palestinian refugees from Syria. There also were allegations of violation of non-refoulement, one of the central pillars of the Temporary Protection Circular, as well as reports of forced relocation of urban refugees into refugee camps.[85] These cases appear to have increased since Turkey reached a deal with the EU in November 2015 to stem the flow of Syrian refugees.[86]

Furthermore, heads of some international nongovernmental organizations continued to complain about encoun-
tering difficulties in registering their organizations with the
government and that the process of registration was very
vague and ambiguous. There also were complaints, especially from Syrian NGOs, that local government officials frequently fined them for employing personnel without work
permits.[87] Simultaneously, NGO staff as well as local government officials complained about a flood of small NGOs,
often with no more than an office and a door bell, seeking
to benefit from the situation for personal gain. Difficulties
of coordination and especially duplication of tasks were also
raised as challenges that required attention to better manage
the needs of urban refugees.

THE LONG RUN AND BURDEN SHARING

Given the extensive destruction in Syria and the absence of
prospects for an immediate political solution to the conflict,
there is a broad-based recognition in Jordan, Lebanon, and
Turkey that Syrian refugees are not likely to be able to return
home for a long time. However, the issue of the refugees'
long-term status is unclear. In these three host countries the
refugees are generally referred to as "guests" and left in a gray
zone in terms of their rights and the level of protection they
can enjoy in the long run.[88] None of the traditional "durable
solutions"—in the form of voluntary return, integration into
host societies, or resettlement—has been available to them.
In the meantime, the Syrian conflict is entering its sixth
year and many of the refugees have been away from their
homes for years. Some of the urban refugees in neighboring
countries are slowly but surely integrating themselves into
local communities. Babies are being born; marriages with

local people are occurring; some of the refugees are building new lives even if their future in all three countries remains legally precarious and economically vulnerable.[89] In effect, some Syrian refugees in Turkish urban settings are no longer refugees waiting for the war to end, but immigrants ready to write a new chapter in their lives.[90] At the same time, many also hope to move on to Europe. Just about half a million of them made their way to the European Union during the course of 2015 in search of a better and more secure future.[91] The journeys to Europe for Syrians and other nationalities have been fraught with difficulties as refugees have had to resort to the services of unscrupulous smugglers, and more than 3,770 deaths have occurred as a result of accidents in the Aegean and Mediterranean Seas.

The refugees face a wide range of challenges in the long run. Once again, there are both similarities and differences across Jordan, Lebanon, and Turkey. One common challenge is how to cope with tension associated with the refugees' long-term presence in host countries. The publics of all three countries resist the notion that refugees may have to become a permanent part of their host communities; the idea of their eventually becoming citizens is unacceptable. In Jordan and Lebanon, integration presents a problem particularly because of the countries' small populations and limited national resources. In the case of Turkey, however, the challenge is more of a cultural one. First of all, Turkey has never before received and integrated Arab refugees or immigrants. Furthermore, the presence of Arab refugees in some parts of the country is a source of resentment toward the current government and is seen as part of an effort to Islamize the country.

Nevertheless, in Turkey, in spite of the absence of a comprehensive governmental policy toward integration, signs of a piecemeal policy have emerged with respect to education and employment. Employment is seen as an important avenue to informal integration but also inclusion in local communities.[92] As Syrian refugees have seen their savings disappear, they have been forced, as mentioned earlier, to find illegal employment in various sectors of the economy ranging from agriculture to the construction sector and the textiles industry. The number of Syrians illegally employed in Turkey in 2015 was put at around 300,000, while the number of actual work permits issued for Syrians was a mere 3,900.[93] Many Syrian entrepreneurs brought their businesses to Turkey and provided employment to both refugees and locals. However, being able to work legally in the country will be critical for the integration of Syrian refugees in Turkey. As one Syrian refugee starkly captured it, employment, like education, is a security issue. He noted "how refugees who are left jobless and without means of survival can become the devil. They can turn into [pro-Assad militants] or join the likes of Jabhat al-Nusra and IS. Providing them with employment allows them to reintegrate into society and gives them hope for a better life."[94]

In principle, the Temporary Protection Circular gives registered refugees the right to seek legal employment in Turkey. Before the general elections in June 2015, the government had prepared legislation to open parts of the national economy to formal employment for Syrian refugees.[95] This was a huge step forward for supporting the incorporation of the Syrian refugees into Turkish society in a more constructive manner. This step also was encouraged by representatives of local business associations in the provinces close to the Syrian border, who argued that there was a shortage of labor in the region. The proposed legislation addressed the problem of "negative coping strategies" that leave Syrian refugees vulnerable to exploitation and abuse. It enabled Syrian skilled workers, such as orthodontists, engineers, teachers, and nurses, to contribute to the Turkish economy and society.[96] The legislation was stalled for much of 2015 because of the country's two parliamentary elections, but it was revived, and finally adopted, after the governing party won a decisive victory in the November elections.[97]

A recent report supported by the Turkish Confederation of Employer Associations drew attention to the need to recognize that Syrians are not about to return and that "the matter at hand has come to a phase that demands transition from emergency support policies to those of integration."[98] The report, based on interviews with leading business representatives, highlights the demand for a comprehensive strategy to integrate Syrian refugees with particular emphasis on the need for education and regulating their access to employment.

Instead, the frustrating deadlock over legal access to labor markets during 2015 pushed refugees into moving toward European Union countries. Granting formal access to the labor market would also help considerably to reduce the current level of expense that the government incurs for the upkeep of the refugees. Most important, it would help empower the refugees in camps and get them out of the passive state of existence—the result of their dependency on government and international handouts.

Conflicting Priorities in Jordan

The Jordanian government strictly prohibits the employment of Syrian refugees and penalizes violators by deporting them.[99] Furthermore, the government does not allow any vocational projects or training programs to equip refugees with marketable skills. Nevertheless, refugees do work illegally and often take up positions that local workers do not fill. At the same time, the government is also concerned that better-trained and skilled Syrian refugees displace local Jordanians from jobs.[100] A study conducted by the International Labor Organization in 2014 noted that the level of unemployment among Jordanians had increased from 14 percent to 22 percent since the arrival of refugees from Syria.[101] The study also estimated that half of the Syrian men living outside camps were informally employed. Yet, at the same time, a prominent Jordanian economist also noted that "only 4 percent of Jordanians compete for low-skilled jobs that refugees would be employed in."[102] These are menial jobs traditionally filled by foreign workers, most from Egypt, Sudan, and Yemen.

The government is caught between conflicting priorities. On the one hand it needs to be sensitive to public opinion in a country that experiences high unemployment. Yet at the same time, similar to its Turkish counterpart, it faces another dilemma: frustrated and unemployed young refugees risk becoming a security challenge.[103] Employment, however, may prolong the stay of refugees and increase the likelihood of their integration in a Jordan that is already sensitive about the demographic balance in the country.

Despite these conflicting concerns, the cutbacks in subsidies for health services and food clearly need to be addressed. This has led the Jordanian government to enlist the help of the UN in opening some sectors of the Jordanian economy to refugee labor with the proviso that the arrangement should create new jobs rather than displace Jordanian workers.[104] The government, as of early 2016, continued to explore the idea of opening the construction, domestic work, agriculture, and textiles sectors to employment while supporting Jordan's industrialization efforts as part of a "holistic approach" to managing the refugee crisis.[105] The competing considerations clearly capture the difficulties that accompany policymaking for the long term.

Additional Challenges in Lebanon

The situation in Lebanon is similar to the one in Jordan, with the exception that the ratio of Syrian refugees to the local population is much higher. This in itself creates additional challenges. Otherwise, as in Jordan, economic and employment-related considerations are critical to the refugees' long-term presence in Lebanon. In this respect, one challenge is the generally held belief that Syrian refugees are forcing wages down, causing greater unemployment, and increasing the number of Lebanese living below the poverty line.[106] Yet, in the economic realm the inflow of humanitarian aid amounting to roughly $800 million has been calculated to have had significant positive multiplier effect on the Lebanese economy.[107] Even so, this effect needs to be balanced against the decline of income from tourism, trade, and investments resulting from the crisis in Syria. An International Labor Organization study in 2014 noted that nearly one-half of the working-age Syrian refugees were economically active in Lebanon and were "engaged in agriculture or in personal and domestic services and, on a smaller scale, in construction. These jobs provide little income and no security or protection, reflecting refugees' low skill capacities."[108] In the meantime, however, Lebanese authorities have become much stricter about employment prospects for Syrian refugees as well as their stay in the country. Concerns about the likely political impact on Lebanon of such a sizeable Syrian refugee community are driving these measures. One commentator described the presence of the large refugee population as creating "a social and political ticking bomb, particularly in relation to the identity and existence of the Lebanese entity."[109] Therefore, the combination of economic and political considerations makes the prospects of improving the inclusion of Syrian refugees into mainstream Lebanese society an even greater challenge than in Jordan and Turkey.

Education also is critical for ensuring better inclusion of Syrian refugees into local communities. The fact that Syria shares a common language with Lebanon and Jordan makes the process of inclusion much easier than in Turkey. Syrian refugees in Turkey, unless they are Turcoman, face the added challenge of having to operate in a completely different linguistic environment, not to mention the complications of deciphering different scripts in everyday life. Jordan and Lebanon opened their national education system to the refugee children. Even so, Syrians in Lebanon face a challenge because the language of instruction is usually in French or English, with Arabic being taught in parallel.[110] Nonetheless, both countries introduced double shifts at schools to accommodate the children.

The experience of Turkey has been much more complicated and problematic. The need to provide education was recognized at a relatively early stage. Initially, however, a rather fragmented and poorly coordinated policy on education emerged based on the premise that the refugees were in Turkey temporarily. Refugee children in camps acquired early access to schooling based on a modified Syrian curriculum in Arabic accompanied by language classes in Turkish. In urban settings, the government permitted children whose parents had residence permits to access Turkish schools while Syrian-run schools, called Temporary Education Centers, emerged but had little governmental supervision. Concerns increased about the content and quality of the education, especially with respect to religious teaching. These concerns finally led the Ministry of Education to implement a much-needed policy to bring all informal Syrian schools under its supervision.[111] At the same time, in June 2015 the ministry was preparing its own schools in the border areas to accommodate Syrian children into second shifts and follow a curriculum to the ones in refugee camps.[112] Furthermore, parents who are registered under the Temporary Protection Circular now have the option of sending their children to Turkish schools as well.

In all three countries the greatest challenge is that only a fraction of the school-age children actually access or attend school regularly; for instance, only a third of the 621,000 school-age Syrian refugee children are in school in Turkey.[113] The situation is not much better in Lebanon and Jordan. Economic difficulties, and the "negative coping mechanisms" they have adopted for livelihood, keep children from attending schools regularly. Yet a Turkish education official acknowledged: "Whether the refugees stay or return to Syria, we simply cannot afford to allow for a lost generation," adding that "without a chance of education, they risk falling victim to radical and terrorist groups."[114] This need to avoid a "lost generation" should be emphasized, since most Syrian children inside Syria are not in school, and the country's future may well depend on the education received by Syrian children outside the country. In this regard, there is closer cooperation with UNICEF in the three countries to develop and fund programs to reach a larger number of Syrian refugees. There is also broad recognition that education is critical to any prospects for integration into host societies. However, it is difficult to see how this situation can be improved unless Syrian refugees also are given access to livelihood opportunities so they can afford to send their children to school rather than rely on the income they can seek out in the streets or through child labor. Similarly, host countries will need considerable support to meet the costs associated with infrastructure and capacity building.

In the long run, ensuring the integration of the refugees would be a "win-win" for all involved: Syria, especially after the war is brought to an end; the three host countries; and the international community. Host countries will need to recognize that integration does not necessarily mean that refugees will never return to their native lands. Instead, access to education and livelihood opportunities is much more likely to provide the basis of "sustainable return" when the day comes than if the refugees remain completely dependent on handouts and are forced into a state of passivity.[115]

However, it would be unfair to expect miracles from the host countries if left to their own devices. These countries are actually providing the international community with a "public good." Protection of refugees is considered to be an international responsibility, one that demands burden-sharing. As discussed in the introduction of this book, so far burden sharing in the form of refugee resettlement from the host countries and funding to meet the needs of refugees has been disappointing. The UN, in its Regional Refugee and Resilience Plan for 2015–16, has recognized that local communities hosting refugees also deserve assistance, and it budgeted for projects to increase the resilience of these communities. This is a very positive step; however, it is disappointing that UN budgets remain seriously underfunded. It is paramount that the international community finds better ways to share the cost of projects with the host countries and also contribute global expertise in addressing the challenges of providing education and employment opportunities for Syrian refugees.

Burden sharing is also critical in terms of legitimizing the expenses of the government in the eyes of the host countries' publics, and it demonstrates that caring for the refugees is an international responsibility and that these countries are not alone. However, in turn the host governments, when presenting the expenditure that they have made for the Syrian refugees, would earn the trust of the international community if they acknowledged that funds do come from abroad—even if not at the desired level. These funds help meet at least some of the needs of the refugees, provide jobs for local nationals, and contribute to the local economy. International agencies and nongovernmental organizations often use these funds to buy local products, pay local taxes on them, and pay the salaries of local employees. Yet, hosting more than 4.5 million refugees has indeed called for great sacrifices from host countries. Measuring that sacrifice is of course difficult and complicated, if not outright impossible, even for economic costs alone.

It is clear that whatever the actual cost for Lebanon, Jordan, and Turkey, the financial assistance from the international community has fallen well short of what is needed. Ankara puts the direct cost of caring for the refugees at $7.6 to $8 billion, Amman at $ 4.5 billion by 2016, and Beirut at more than $4 billion so far.[116] On the other hand, a World Bank assessment put the overall cost of the Syrian crisis at

$35 billion through mid-2014 without including the actual cost of caring for the refugees.[117] As noted in the introductory chapter, the Syrian crisis has received a disproportionate percentage of global humanitarian funds. Even so, the $15 billion that the international community has committed or spent in the form of assistance since the beginning of the crisis falls well short of meeting the needs of the Syrian displaced and refugees.[118]

The European refugee crisis, discussed below, has drawn attention to the plight of Syrian refugees in neighboring countries and accentuated the need for greater recognition of the burden carried by these countries. This has led to several positive developments. The European Union and the United States have agreed to increase their funding for programs to address the needs of Syrian refugees in the region. After long and arduous negotiations late in November 2015 the EU and Turkey formally adopted an "Action Plan" that will make more than 3 billion euros available for supporting Syrian refugees in Turkey.[119] Total funding for UN budgets for Syria has edged up from less than one-fourth in midsummer to a little over half by the end of 2015.[120] Britain has also taken the lead to call for a major "Syrian Donors Conference" in February 2016.[121] Furthermore, the Group of 20 Leaders' Communique adopted at the summit in Antalya, Turkey, in mid-November 2015 included a paragraph calling on the leaders "to continue further strengthening our support for all efforts to provide protection and assistance and to find durable solutions for the unprecedented numbers of refugees and internally displaced persons in various parts of the world" including Syria.[122] There were also calls emphasizing that protecting and assisting the refugees was a global responsibility that should be distributed more equally. However, it will be critical to translate these developments into actual projects to benefit both Syrian refugees as well as their host communities.

Similarly, the international community has not been particularly generous with respect to resettlement. In spite of numerous appeals by United Nations High Commissioner for Refugees Antonio Guterres to the EU and the United States to offer more resettlement places available, only about 125,000 spots were available as of December 2015. That number represented less than 3 percent of all Syrian refugees.[123] It was the arrival by September 2015 of more than half a million Syrian refugees and others by sea that forced the EU to respond.[124] In September the EU decided to resettle 160,000 refugees among EU member countries but did not make places available for taking refugees directly from the major refugee-hosting countries.[125] Britain, which had accepted fewer than 5,000 Syrian refugees since 2011, promised to admit 20,000 more refugees in the next five years from countries neighboring Syria.[126] France also announced that it would make its 24,000 quota available in the next two years for resettling Syrian refugees from the neighboring countries.[127] The Action Plan adopted between the EU and Turkey referred vaguely to making places available for resettlement of Syrian refugees from the countries of the region.[128] Time will tell whether a subsequent EU "voluntary admissions" program to resettle Syrian refugees from Turkey will work.[129] However, the fact that as of early 2016 only 272 refugees were relocated from Greece and Italy on the basis of the deal reached among EU members was not very promising for the future of this "voluntary" scheme.[130]

The EU-Turkey Action Plan was intended to provide much more support for host countries and for Turkey in particular. The plan promised to share the cost of the refugees' upkeep, access to public services, and their participation in local economies. In return, Turkey was expected to prevent the smuggling into the EU of Syrian refugees and other migrants. EU leaders, ranging from German chancellor Angela Merkel to the European Commission vice president Frans Timmermans and the European commissioner Johannes Hahn, stressed the importance of cooperating with Turkey to stem the flow of refugees into Europe and promised the prospect of introducing visa-free travel for Turkish nationals as well as revitalizing negotiations for Turkey's long-delayed accession into EU membership.[131] However, the plan also received considerable criticism for being focused primarily on addressing the interests of the EU and Turkey rather than the welfare of Syrian refugees. Critics also noted that it was based on a transactional "we pay, you keep the refugees" logic, with little regard for ethical and value issues.[132] Amnesty International was particularly critical of the plan; its report noted in detail that denying the refugees the possibility to seek protection in Europe would fall short of forging a durable solution to the crisis.[133]

The European refugee crisis is still evolving. By the end of 2015, the number of arrivals had reached more than one million (see figure 2-2). More than one-half of these refugees are Syrians, some of whom came directly from Syria via Turkey and some of whom left the countries hosting Syrian refugees.[134] In any event, many experts now recognize that lack of adequate international solidarity in sharing the burden of managing the Syrian refugees was a major and compelling reason why Syrians began to flee to Europe in massive numbers. In that respect, it is significant that the refugees who were interviewed on why they decided to attempt to get to Europe cited the desire to ensure the education of their children and the lack of access to labor markets.[135] These happen to be two areas with which the hosting

FIGURE 2-2. *Irregular Migrant and Refugee Arrivals into Europe by Sea, by Country of Origin, 2015*

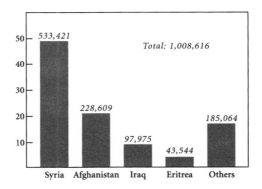

Source: United Nations High Commissioner of Refugees, "Refugees/Migrants Emergency Response Plan."

countries neighboring Syria have struggled the most and have failed to make significant progress. Substantive and effective international assistance might have produced a different result. Furthermore, the absence of any prospects for a legal path for moving on to third countries encouraged many Syrians to resort to human smugglers. It is not surprising that many struggled for years in neighboring countries, lost hope about the future, and finally resorted to a form of "self-resettling" themselves to Europe.

Managing a mass influx of refugees in such a short period of time and then integrating those who have been recognized as refugees will be a mammoth task. Germany has been at the forefront in receiving the bulk of the refugees, and German chancellor Angela Merkel has received wide international praise—but also much domestic criticism—for her stand.[136] However, the fact that some of the perpetrators of the November 2015 attacks in Paris appear to have entered Europe through Greece has further complicated the man-

agement of the refugee crisis. There already have been calls
that measures introduced to ensure public security across
Europe should not work to the detriment of refugees and
that borders should definitely not be closed. Such measures
would undermine the prospects of future resettlement from
host countries and make the situation even more precarious
for refugees in flight. At the same time, there are also wor-
ries that the pressure to cope with the crisis could risk the
unraveling of the EU itself, while others have been critical
of the EU's selfishness and failure to live up to its values.[137]

Security concerns subsequent to the Paris attacks and
the December 2015 attack in San Bernardino, California,
have destroyed the good will that emerged in the United
States in support of receiving Syrian refugees, which had
been the initial response to a widely published photograph
of the body of a little boy on a Turkish beach in September
2015. The reaction to San Bernardino was swift, with a large
group of governors announcing their opposition to the resettlement of any Syrian refugees in their states.[138] The U.S.
House of Representatives passed a bill calling for even more
onerous security restrictions on Syrian refugees. This rhetoric is particularly disappointing because it came at a time
when the U.S. administration had just committed itself to
admitting 10,000 Syrian refugees before the end of October
2016, as well as expanding the annual general resettlement
quota from 70,000 to 100,000 in the coming years.[139] These
steps were particularly welcomed by advocates, because previously the United States had been slow in admitting Syrian
refugees and was facing criticism from refugee advocacy
groups. Fewer than 2,200 Syrians have been resettled in the
United States since the war's outbreak in 2011.[140]

The absence of effective burden sharing had played an
important role in Turkey's call for safe zones in Syria—an

issue discussed in more detail in the next chapter. Turkey has pushed the idea on numerous occasions since 2012, when the number of Syrian refugees first crossed the 100,000 "red line" once declared by the government.[141] The Turkish government has frequently sought support for safe zones from the United States and the EU. In July 2015, upon signing an agreement with the United States to coordinate its military effort against ISIS, Turkey advocated the establishment of such a zone within the so-called ISIS-free area north of Aleppo, stretching about sixty miles along the Syrian-Turkish border.[142] Due to Washington's continued resistance, however, this safe zone was never realized.[143] The idea was subsequently revived by the president of Turkey during the November 2015 G-20 summit but did not receive much support from U.S. president Barack Obama.[144] Nor was the idea embraced by the EU, which was itself struggling with unprecedented refugee arrivals.[145] Because of European reluctance, the creation of a safe zone was dropped from the agenda of the EU-Turkey summit of late November. In any event, the Turkish downing of a Russian fighter plane in late November 2015 brought the prospects of a safe zone to an end. Russia's introduction of powerful ballistic missiles into Syria has ironically created a de facto no-fly zone in reverse.[146] The Turkish idea of a safe zone in Syria across from the Turkish border may well be dead for the foreseeable future.

We turn now to an examination of some of the challenges posed by those displaced—and trapped—inside Syrian borders.

CHAPTER 3

Communities at Risk inside Syria

*The Internally Displaced, Palestinians, Besieged,
and Other Trapped Populations*

While much of the world's attention has focused, perhaps understandably, on the exodus of Syrian refugees fleeing their country, less attention has been paid to those displaced within the country and even less to those who are unable to leave their communities. This chapter looks at the dynamics of internal displacement within Syria and at the plight of those who for various reasons are unable to move. We then turn to the extremely complicated issue of how to assist and protect civilians within the borders of their own country. In particular, this chapter addresses issues of cross-border assistance to areas not under the control of the government and to the potential for safe areas, no-fly zones, humanitarian corridors, and other forms of humanitarian intervention to provide assistance to those affected by the Syrian conflict who remain within Syria's borders.

INTERNALLY DISPLACED PEOPLE

While the protection of those people who flee across international borders is the responsibility of the governments that host them, with the support of the United Nations High Commissioner for Refugees (UNHCR), the responsibility for protecting those displaced within their own countries falls to their national governments. In the UN's legal jargon, these people are known as "internally displaced persons," or IDPs.

The primary role of the state is clear in principle, recognized both in international law and regularly reaffirmed in international statements of principle. Most notably, United Nations Resolution 46/182 of 1991, on "Strengthening the Coordination of Humanitarian Assistance," which remains the normative basis for international humanitarian action, states:

> The sovereignty, territorial integrity and national unity of States must be fully respected in accordance with the Charter of the United Nations. In this context, humanitarian assistance should be provided with the consent of the affected country and in principle on the basis of an appeal by the affected country.
>
> Each State has the responsibility first and foremost to take care of victims of natural disasters and other emergencies occurring on its territory. Hence, the affected State has the primary role in the initiation, organization, coordination, and implementation of humanitarian assistance within its territory.[1]

One of the great human rights achievements of the past two decades has been the recognition that the rights of those displaced within their borders need to be protected; this recognition has been accompanied by the development of a normative framework to affirm those rights. The *Guiding Principles on Internal Displacement* affirm that the state has primary responsibility for protecting the rights of IDPs and that IDPs should expect their government to fulfil this responsibility toward them. The document then proceeds to spell out the rights of IDPs and consequent responsibilities of the authorities in all phases of displacement: protection from arbitrary displacement, protection and assistance during displacement, and securing solutions to displacement.[2] The *Guiding Principles* specify that humanitarian organizations have a right to offer assistance, that consent to such offers should not be arbitrarily withheld, and that authorities should ensure "rapid and unimpeded" access to the displaced.

The *Guiding Principles* were affirmed in the World Summit Outcome Document of 2005, in which 186 heads of state unanimously reiterated the primary responsibility of states to address internal displacement and affirmed the *Guiding Principles* as "an important international framework for the protection of internally displaced persons."[3] In the same World Summit Outcome Document the international community also endorsed the concept of the "responsibility to protect," known as R2P, which described a collective international responsibility to protect people from genocide, war crimes, and other crimes against humanity. This was no mere coincidence: The idea of a responsibility to protect was inspired by and emerged from efforts throughout the 1990s to design an effective international response to protect IDPs based on the concept of "sovereignty as responsibility."[4] While it is beyond the scope of this study to trace the ups and (mostly) downs of the implementation of R2P, suffice it to say that the concept has not been applied in Syria in spite of the fact that war crimes and widespread atrocities have been unambiguously documented. Nor has the Syrian government exercised its responsibilities to protect and assist IDPs and to facilitate the "rapid and unimpeded access to the displaced."

Moreover, the fact that the Syrian government is carrying out widespread and increasingly lethal attacks on civilian areas highlights a fundamental contradiction in international law: The same authorities that cause displacement are also responsible for protecting and assisting those displaced by their actions. While Syria is certainly not the only government in this position, the sheer scale of both internal displacement and well-documented atrocities in Syria highlight the inherent contradictions in the way IDPs are treated in international law.[5]

INTERNAL DISPLACEMENT IN SYRIA

There have been examples of large-scale displacement in Syria's recent history—most notably in Hama in 1982 when the government forced some 250,000 people from their homes and killed more than 25,000 in a campaign to suppress protests by the Muslim Brotherhood.[6] More displacements resulted since 2006 from a devastating drought. Historically, however, rates of rural-urban migration have been relatively low in Syria. Rather, in spite of authoritarian domestic and bellicose foreign policies, Syria was known as a generous and welcoming host for Palestinian and Iraqi refugees.

Since the eruption of violence in March 2011, an increasing number of people have been displaced from their homes, the vast majority of whom remain within Syrian borders. Much more is known about the 4-plus million refugees in neighboring countries than about the almost 6.5 million IDPs. While governments or the UNHCR have established systems to register refugees in all the neighboring countries, the Syrian government has no such registration mechanism inside the country. Access by UN agencies to the internally displaced is both limited and sporadic. The Office for the Coordination of Humanitarian Affairs (OCHA) is the UN body responsible for compiling data on the number of IDPs and in October 2015 estimated their number as 6.5 million IDPs—a figure that has declined since the high of 7.6 million in October 2014, perhaps reflecting the increase in people fleeing the country.[7] OCHA began reporting on IDP estimates only in January 2013 and has only updated the figure four times since then.[8] In contrast, UNHCR reports refugee numbers on a regular basis, usually weekly. While refugee estimates generally show a fairly direct linear trend, numbers of IDPs seem to lurch upward in stepwise fashion. As of late 2015, the governorates (provinces) with the most IDPs were Aleppo (1.2 million), Rural Damascus (1.269 million), and Idlib (705,000).[9] These IDPs are part of a larger group of 13.5 million estimated to be in need of humanitarian assistance (see figure 3-1).[10]

The stepwise movements in IDP numbers reflects the difficulties in compiling such numbers as well as the inherently political nature of coming up with estimates of IDPs in a highly volatile context. When their situation worsens, people go to stay with relatives in another part of the country and then move back (or move somewhere else) in response to local security issues. The Internal Displacement Monitoring Centre (IDMC) in Switzerland, the world's leading authority on IDP data, further notes that different methodologies are used by different actors and in different parts of Syria.[11] The figures presented by OCHA are in fact triangulated

FIGURE 3-1. *Internally Displaced Persons, 2013–15*

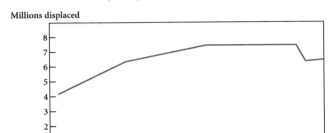

Millions displaced

Source: United Nations Office for the Coordination of Humanitarian Affairs

between statistics collected by the Syrian government, the Syrian Arab Red Crescent Society, and OCHA. But none of these actors has access to some parts of Syria, and those are areas likely to have high rates of internal displacement. The Syrian government (like governments in other parts of the world) has an interest in minimizing the extent of internal displacement and argues that humanitarian agencies inflate their estimates for political reasons.

Even in using the figure of 6.5 million IDPs, it must be emphasized that this is a very rough estimate, particularly given the dynamic nature of displacement. For example, IDMC reported that the conflict newly displaced as many as 1.2 million Syrians in 2014.[12] Even in the midst of the conflict, some people are able to return to their homes. Thus the United States Agency for International Development cited UN reports that as of mid-September 2015, more than 3,000 households, 80 percent of them Palestinian, had returned to the Husseinieh neighborhood in Damascus two years after they had been displaced by armed conflict.[13]

Given both the direct and indirect effects of the conflict, millions of Syrians have left their communities in search of safety and survival. Displacement in Syria, as elsewhere, is a dynamic process. Many people have been displaced multiple times. People return to their homes to check on property and relatives, they go to stay with relatives in areas perceived as safer and then move on when conditions deteriorate. There is a clear relationship between internal displacement and refugee movements. As a Jordanian Foreign Ministry official stated, "Jordan is typically the fourth stop for Syrians; most of the refugees arriving have been previously displaced at least three times inside Syria."[14]

For those displaced within Syria, shelter is an immediate and serious concern. In 2014 analysts estimated that 30 percent of the country's housing stock had been destroyed—and there have been widespread aerial bombardments since then.[15] The overwhelming majority of IDPs (85 percent) stay with relatives or friends or rent accommodations in the communities where they arrive.[16] But when resources run out or when IDPs have no relatives or friends to stay with, they seek alternative accommodations by living in abandoned property, in makeshift shelters, or even in caves. According to Syrian government reports in 2013, only 4 percent of IDPs in the country were living in collective shelters.[17]

Compared to refugees who have made it out of the country, those displaced within Syria are probably more vulnerable because they are closer to the violence, less likely to be assessed and counted, and less likely to have access to international assistance. Older people, for example, are probably less able to travel far from home. While people over 65 made up some 6 percent of Syria's pre-war population, they account for only 1.6 percent of registered refugees.[18] Perhaps because women are able to move more freely through checkpoints or because men have been killed or are fighting, most IDPs are women and girls. While IDPs have been taken in by host families and communities, in some places the sheer number of IDPs seeking safety has increased tensions. Even in official camps, sudden influxes of IDPs may overwhelm services. Health services and education for children are largely absent, and children are experiencing clear signs of trauma.[19] In 2013 reports were that half of IDP children had dropped out of school—a figure that seems to have remained constant.[20] In 2015 OCHA reported that in addition to those already out of school another 25 percent of children were at risk of dropping out.[21]

IDPs face serious protection needs related to the ongoing conflict. Many people have lost identity and other documents, and without them crossing checkpoints is risky. One-half of the civil affairs departments in the country have been destroyed, hampering the replacement of documentation.[22] Families have been separated, there is a heightened risk of sexual violence, and children are at risk. IDPs and refugee women report increased domestic violence and pressure to resort to negative coping methods such as early marriage and prostitution.[23] IDPs living in makeshift camps near the Turkish border have been attacked.[24] The proliferation of small arms and the widespread presence of mines, explosive remnants of war, and unexploded ordnance pose a particular threat for children. Children have been used as human shields and recruited into armed forces, in particular by armed opposition groups, while in Lebanon some reportedly have engaged in armed hostilities.[25] IDPs also face risks because of the loss of social networks that can protect people in conflict situations by providing guidance on issues such as who can be trusted and what are the safe routes through the country or city.

There is no legal or policy framework for IDPs in Syria.[26] In fact, the Syrian government does not acknowledge that there are IDPs in the country. Rather, according to the 2013 report of the UN's Special Rapporteur on the Human Rights of IDPs, "the Government stated its position that the Syrian Arab Republic was not suffering from a phenomenon called 'internally displaced persons' but rather had been subject to a series of terrorist attacks undertaken by armed outlaws. As such, persons being assisted were referred to as 'people who left their homes as a result of the current events.'"[27]

While all IDPs in Syria are at risk, specific groups have experienced particularly high risk, including the Palestinian and Iraqi refugees, religious minorities, and Kurds.

Palestinian and Iraqi Refugees

Palestinian and Iraqi refugees have been particularly vulnerable. The UN's agency for the Palestinians—the United Nations Relief and Works Agency (UNRWA)—reports that all twelve Palestinian refugee camps and all 560,000 registered Palestinian refugees in Syria have been affected by the war. The majority of the 450,000 refugees remaining in Syria are internally displaced and in need of humanitarian assistance. One-third of UNRWA facilities in Syria have been damaged or destroyed, and UNRWA reports that the civilian character of the camps and neutrality is no longer respected.[28] This is a breach of international law under which refugees are protected during armed conflict, in all circumstances and without adverse distinction.[29]

The destruction of homes in Palestine refugee camps, the violence, the loss of livelihoods, and the exhaustion of savings and assets have forced many Palestinians living in Syria to leave their communities—but they have been turned back at borders when they have tried to escape the country. Jordan has denied entry to most Palestinians since the beginning of the crisis, and in May 2014 Lebanon imposed restrictions on Palestinians' entry. All together around 80,000 Palestinian refugees from Syria have been displaced across international borders, including 42,500 in Lebanon and 16,000 in Jordan. Those who have sought protection in neighboring countries experience marginalization and acute vulnerability and are unable to access civil registration procedures and basic social services.[30]

Yarmouk, a Palestinian refugee camp near Damascus, was established by the Syrian government in 1957 and by the time the present conflict broke out in 2011 was home to 150,000–200,000 Palestinians as well as some 650,000 Syrians. In 2012 intense fighting broke out in the camp between pro-regime and opposition forces, with the Free Syrian Army and the al-Nusra Front taking control of the camp by the end of the year. Those who could, left. The Syrians living in Yarmouk mainly went to stay with relatives and friends in central Damascus or other cities or moved to Lebanon or Jordan. But the Palestinians in the camp had fewer options. In mid-2013 the government imposed an almost total siege, prohibiting the entry or exit from the camp of all but a few emergency medical cases. All twenty-eight schools in the camp were closed, electricity was shut off, and food and medical supplies were in short supply. A news article in *The Guardian* cited a report by a Palestinian woman from Yarmouk that at the worst point of the siege a kilo of rice cost about 120 times more there than in central Damascus (prices later fell sharply in both places).[31] The siege was "relaxed" in January 2014, and although there were some ad hoc aid deliveries during 2014, access remained extremely limited. ISIS attacked the camp in April 2015. Although its control was short-lived, the camp remains under the control of opposition groups with the government controlling the entrance to the camp. In July 2015 the UN took Yarmouk off its list of besieged areas, but the conflict remains intense and access is extremely limited. For example, UNRWA has been unable to access the camp's interior since March 28, 2015. An estimated 5,000–8,000 inhabitants remain in the Yarmouk camp, and, as of September 2015, typhoid had broken out.[32]

Iraqi refugees in Syria also have been affected by the conflict. In 2012 UNHCR reported that there were over 400,000 Iraqi refugees in Syria (although only 62,000 were reported as receiving assistance from UNHCR).[33] With the escalation of the conflict, at least 100,000 Iraqis are reported to have returned to Iraq from Syria, further complicating the situation in northern Iraq where they join large numbers of Iraqi IDPs and Syrian refugees in a part of the country facing serious political pressures.[34]

Religious Minorities

As noted in the introductory chapter, most of the victims of the Syrian war, including most of those displaced, are Sunni Muslims—and yet the impact of displacement on minorities is significant, given their relatively smaller percentage of the population. The increasingly sectarian nature of the conflict is reflected in patterns of displacement. In its August 2015 report, the Independent International Commission of Inquiry on the Syrian Arab Republic stated: "As communities and groups are, or feel, threatened, they have retreated into areas where they believe themselves to be more protected. This has further strengthened the dangerous perception of a link between some ethnicities and/or religions and political allegiances. Consequently, indiscriminate attacks on areas held by an opposing warring party are increasingly likely to affect specific religious or ethnic communities."[35]

There is little reliable information about how many Alawites have been internally displaced, but anecdotal evidence suggests that those who did not already live in Alawite-majority areas have fled to what they believe to be safer areas within Syria.[36] Regardless of sect, most Syrians with the means to do so have already left the country, and the Alawites are likely no exception. However, UNHCR reports that very few people from minorities have registered as refugees in Jordan, and even in Lebanon (which has its own Alawite community) minorities fear registering due to concerns about retribution from other refugees.[37] A small number of Alawites have reportedly fled to Turkey to seek shelter with their co-religionists, Turkey's Alawite community, and have gone to cities where the opposition party, the Republican People's Party, runs municipalities.[38] As the conflict has become more sectarian, Syrian Alawites have avoided the Sunni-dominated border camps and fled to areas such as Istanbul, where one local NGO estimated in late 2013 that there were approximately 3,000 Syrian Alawites, hundreds of them homeless. Spillover from the Syrian conflict has also reportedly increased tensions between Turkey's Alawite minority and Turkish Sunnis in Hatay province, which borders Syria and was part of its territory until 1939.[39]

There also is little reliable information about the number of Christians who have fled Syria. While most Syrian Christians are thought to have joined their co-religionists in Lebanon, media reports suggest that a small number have sought sanctuary in Jordan and Turkey.[40] In mid-2013 Turkish officials announced they were building a tented camp with a capacity of 2,500 in Midyat, a town in Mardin province near the Syrian border, to house Christian refugees.[41] Turkey has a small Assyrian minority living in the same area. By the end of the year, about a hundred Syrian Christian families had reportedly fled to the Mardin area, but it is unclear how many were actually living in the camp.[42] Some Syrian Christians have sought sanctuary with church communities in Istanbul.[43] However, not all Syrian Christians are counting on Turkish hospitality. In February 2015 the Syrian Catholic archbishop of the conflict-torn region of Hassakeh accused Turkey of preventing Christians from fleeing Syria while allowing ISIS fighters to cross the border unchecked.[44]

Small numbers of ethnic Armenians from Syria have also sought refuge in Turkey.[45] Syria's Christian minority includes about 100,000 people of Armenian descent, mostly centered in the Aleppo area. By mid-2015, it was estimated that around 40,000 Armenians remained in the city. More than 15,000 had left for Armenia, which offered them citizenship.[46] However, many are struggling to make a living in their new home. Up to forty Syrian Armenian families reportedly settled in Nagorno-Karabakh, a disputed region that is part of Azerbaijan but has an ethnic Armenian minority. Armenia has also received Yazidi refugees from Iraq.[47] In March 2013 Islamist rebels seized control of the Syrian-Armenian town of Kassab, which lies near the Turkish border, displacing most of the town's population.[48] Throughout Syria, Armenians have reportedly become targets for kidnapping, extortion, and murder.

One little-known minority group in Syria deeply affected by the civil war are the Dom. They form a distinct linguistic group with links to India and the Roma in Europe. The Dom have traditionally faced discrimination and have also been displaced by the current conflict. Field research suggests that thousands have fled to Turkey and continue to face discrimination there, too.[49]

The Particular Case of Kurdish Displacement inside Syria

The widespread internal displacement in Syria is affecting patterns of both sectarian and ethnic settlement in the country. When people are displaced, they tend to move to areas where their own ethnic group or sect is in a majority (as was the case in Iraq). The case of the Syrian Kurds is particularly interesting in this regard as it demonstrates the relationship between displacement, ethnic/sectarian divisions, the military conflict—and perhaps some of the future possibilities for the country.

Syria's Kurdish population lives near the Turkish and Iraqi borders, although there are also substantial Kurdish populations in Syria's large cities. But unlike northern Iraq, the territory of Kurdish settlement in Syria is not contiguous and does not have the mountainous territory from which an armed insurgency against central rule can be organized. Over the years, the Syrian Kurds were partly co-opted by the regime and their political activities vis à vis Turkey and their smuggling were tolerated. But they have also seethed under systematic discrimination and repression. Some 300,000 Kurds—15 percent of the estimated 2 million Kurds living in Syria—remain stateless. In April 2011 the regime gave citizenship to 150,000 stateless Kurds, but many were unable to benefit from these provisions. Kurds did not give Assad much credit for the grossly overdue measure, but neither did they flock to join the uprising against him.[50]

Traditional Kurdish political parties feared reprisals if they actively joined the opposition even though many young Kurds did so. And the regime for the most part left the Kurds alone.[51] The largest and most influential of the Syrian Kurdish political parties, the Democratic Union Party (Partiya Yekîtiya Demokrat, PYD), perceived as a Syrian-Kurdish offshoot of the militant Kurdistan Workers' Party (PKK) in Turkey, has historically been reluctant to confront the regime, prompting charges of collusion, especially from the Turkish government.[52]

With the conflict and the ensuing displacement, the situation changed as Kurds previously displaced from the region returned to Syria's Kurdish regions in the north; as of October 2012 half of Syria's Kurdish regions were controlled by local Kurdish leaders, including at border points with Iraq's Kurdish autonomous region. By mid-2012 the PYD took advantage of the partial withdrawal of regime forces from Kurdish areas to establish its political and security presence and openly asserted itself as the authority in charge of state institutions in most predominantly Kurdish towns. The only Kurdish political rival to the PYD is a coalition of Kurdish parties aligned with the Kurdistan Regional Government in Iraq. But Kurdish factions compete not only with each other but also with non-Kurdish opposition groups, and most are alienated from the Islamist and Arab nationalist opposition groups (in part because of the dependence of these groups on Turkey and Gulf-based conservative sponsors). Sectarian and ethnic tensions flared up in 2013 between Kurds and Arabs, leading to clashes between the PYD's People's Protection Units (YPG) and the Free Syrian Army.[53] However, in June 2015 PYD and local groups associated with the Free Syrian Army fought together in dislodging ISIS from the border town of Tal Abyad. Since then, in coordination with the United States, Syrian Kurds have been pushing south toward ISIS's stronghold of Raqqa, and there are reports of YPG efforts to displace non-Kurds from the region.[54]

Syrian Kurds have emerged as a major—and probably the most effective—partner of the U.S.-led coalition in its fight against ISIS. The growing cooperation between the U.S. military and the YPG has reportedly angered Turkey, which views the PYD as an affiliate of the PKK and hence as a security threat.[55] The YPG emerged victorious from the long battle over the border towns of Kobane (reportedly with the assistance of Kurdish fighters from Iraq and Turkey) and Tal Abyad. However, along with Kurdish battlefield successes there have been reports of tensions with Arab opposition groups and even accusations that Kurdish forces are involved in ethnic cleansing.[56] In July 2015 the YPG announced that it was now in full control of the city of Hassakeh, with both ISIS and the regime withdrawing. Kurds are also in control of a corner of Syria in the northwest known as Afrin, in this way creating a "Kurdish corridor" along most of Turkey's border with Syria with the exception of a stretch of land west of the Euphrates. The Turkish government considers the prospect of an uninterrupted Kurdish-controlled zone along its border a threat to national security and is vehemently opposed to YPG or PYD crossing the Euphrates to the west.[57] In turn this complicates Turkey's relationship with the United States, which maintains very close cooperation with the PYD in the fight against ISIS.

The fighting in Kurdish areas has also created large-scale displacement. Since July 2012 a steady influx of Syrian Kurds have crossed into Iraq, numbering close to 250,000.[58] In mid-2012 Human Rights Watch reported that most Syrian Kurds in Iraq were fleeing the fighting with opposition groups, as well as conscription and the violence of the regime, although ISIS and other Islamist militant groups have since become the dominant threat rather than Free Syrian Army–affiliated militants.[59]

The arrival of Syrian Kurds has placed considerable pressure on authorities in Iraqi Kurdistan, which is also facing a massive influx of IDPs from elsewhere in Iraq. Despite a shared cultural heritage, tensions have emerged between Syrian Kurdish refugees and the host community. Syrian Kurds were originally given residency and work permits, but as competition increased with Iraqi Kurds for scarce livelihoods, authorities in Erbil and Sulaimaniya suspended the issuing of residency cards and encouraged refugees to move into camps.[60]

As the battle was raging in mid-2015 in the border town of Kobane, UNHCR said that over 170,000 Syrian Kurds had crossed into Turkey.[61] However, the agency said many preferred to continue their journey to the Kurdish region of Iraq or to other areas in Syria. As discussed in chapter 2, in early 2015 Turkish authorities opened a refugee camp in Suruç to accommodate the refugees from Kobane, while some remained housed in camps managed by the municipality.[62]

On July 20, 2015, tensions flared over a suspected ISIS suicide bombing in Suruç, Turkey, which left 32 people dead.[63] Most of those killed were young activists helping to rebuild Kobane, which lies just across the border. Kurdish leaders blamed the Turkish government for failing to take sufficient measures against ISIS. PKK militants have retaliated by killing two Turkish police officers, accusing them of collaborating with ISIS.[64] Also in July 2015, Turkey launched airstrikes against both ISIS and Kurdish targets inside Syria.[65]

The displacement of Kurds to their historical homeland and the establishment of Kurdish parties' control of these areas offer the possibility for the creation of a Kurdish homeland; this is an outcome obviously feared by the Turkish government, which is concerned about the impact of such an outcome on its own Kurdish population.[66] But over the long haul there are likely to be differences among Iraqi Kurdistan—which wants to consolidate a broad, Kurdish-dominated area straddling the Iraqi-Syrian border—and the Syrian Kurdish opposition and Turkey.

Displacement inside Syria thus has direct implications for the future of Kurds in Syria and the region. Internal displacement inside Syria is also linked to the movement of refugees across all of Syria's borders.[67] This phenomenon also likely will have long-range consequences for the region.

AID INSIDE SYRIA

Syria is the most difficult operating environment in the world today for delivery of humanitarian assistance. While funding for humanitarian aid inside Syria is in short supply—and, as discussed in chapter 1, is funded at a lower rate than refugee operations—the main difficulties stem from the hostile policy of the Syrian government, the multitude of armed actors, and the conflict itself. The fact that the battle lines are constantly shifting and different groups exercise control of territories at different times means, for example, that roads that are open one day are closed the next. The limited availability of fuel, the lack of drivers and transportation companies willing to operate in certain areas of the country, and damaged infrastructure are further impediments to delivery of relief items. As a former UN official working in Syria summarized, "To work on humanitarian issues inside Syria is to walk an ethical tightrope."[68]

Even before the conflict, international agencies were viewed with suspicion by the Assad government and faced restrictions on their actions. For example, the few agencies working with Iraqi refugees were forbidden to meet with each other.[69] As the Syrian conflict has escalated, the government has viewed international humanitarian actors with increased suspicion, seeing them as allied with Western interests and as potential "trojan horses" that can collect information to be used for military purposes. After all, military intervention in Libya was justified by the West as a measure to protect civilians.

The regime has imposed numerous bureaucratic obstacles on humanitarian actors working in government-controlled areas and penalties for those working in cross-border operations.[70] Permission to deliver aid to government-controlled areas requires days, sometimes weeks, of advance notice and sign-offs from multiple agencies. The government has been very restrictive about which international organizations it will permit to operate inside its borders. It maintains strict limits on numbers of visas and approves very few local Syrian partners for the international nongovernmental organizations, with the notable exception of the Syrian Arab Red Crescent Society, an auxiliary to the government that is the channel for the vast majority of aid deliveries.[71] Its approval is required for field offices, deployment of staff, and mobilization of convoys, and it is largely responsible for carrying out needs assessments in the country. Its network of some 11,000 volunteers throughout the country is unparalleled. But the Red Crescent Society walks a tightrope. Viewed as agents of the government by some, its staff have also been accused by the government of aiding the rebels, and over fifty of its staff and volunteers have been killed in action.[72] While the Syrian government has begun to allow international agencies to work with other Syrian local partners, many of these are newly formed and lack capacity.[73]

International nongovernmental organizations that run cross-border aid programs are not permitted to work in government-controlled areas, thus forcing them to choose which side to work on. Deliveries of medical supplies have come under particular scrutiny as they are seen as helping the rebels. Even the International Committee of the Red Cross, which has some 300 staff working inside Syria (its largest operation in the world), has not been able to get access to detention centers, a core component of its humanitarian work. The Red Cross, like the UN and other international nongovernmental organizations, has faced frustrating delays in delivering assistance to vulnerable groups.

From time to time agency convoys have been allowed to deliver aid from government-controlled areas to areas that previously had been inaccessible because they are controlled by non-state armed groups. In May 2015 the UN reported that it had requested forty-four such convoys since December 2014, only four of which had been completed.[74] Security-related impediments to access include active fighting and military operations, closure of key access routes, and a proliferation of formal and informal checkpoints. In addition, an increasing number of humanitarian workers and UN staff members have been killed, injured, or kidnapped and attacks on goods and facilities and UN vehicles have multiplied.[75] As of June 2015, seventy-seven humanitarian workers had been killed since the beginning of the conflict, including ten in the first half of 2015.[76] Diversion of aid by both opposition and government forces reportedly is a frequent occurrence. OCHA reported in mid-2015 that access to affected populations decreased in the first half of the year due to a combination of factors, including "insecurity and shifting conflict lines, deliberate interference, restrictions on access and onerous administrative procedures that constrain the effective delivery of assistance."[77]

It is a testament to the commitment of staff and agencies

that aid, insufficient as it is, has been provided inside Syria. The World Food Program provides food aid to 4 million people inside Syria each month, and to another 1.5 million refugees in neighboring countries.[78] But in September 2015 the agency had to cut aid to one-third of refugee beneficiaries due to funding shortfalls.[79] Other UN agencies, such as UNHCR and the UN Population Fund, have provided relief items to Syrians affected by the conflict, but it is hard to assess the impact of this assistance, particularly given the fact that more than 13 million Syrians are estimated to be in need of humanitarian aid and that almost 4.8 million live in what are perhaps euphemistically called "hard-to-reach" areas.

Many of those interviewed for this study were critical of the United Nations' role inside Syria, saying that UN agencies were treading a fine line between being co-opted by the government and maintaining the independence embodied in humanitarian principles. The fear of being expelled from the country was perhaps the driving force in their conciliatory actions vis-à-vis the government. The intense politicization of aid, along with the inability to use traditional monitoring mechanisms and tools in delivery of aid, put tremendous pressure on all agencies. As Ben Parker, former head of OCHA's operations in Syria wrote: "The international system became warped under this onslaught, leading to turf battles and sharp practice, fundraising contradictions, donor interference, double-speak and poor risk management, all the while under intense pressure and micro-management from headquarters and capitals. Any divisions were exploited by government and security agencies."[80]

As discussed further below, UN Security Council resolutions have allowed some cross-border operations, but UN agencies and NGOs involved in cross-border operations were not in contact with those agencies working inside Syria. At the end of 2014, humanitarian partners providing assistance inside Syria—whether operating from Damascus, Turkey, or Jordan—committed themselves to working together in a "Whole of Syria" approach.[81] This initiative brought together more than 270 international and national actors under a comprehensive framework, common response plan, and supporting coordination structure. Interviews with UN staff in Turkey in June 2015 revealed some cautious optimism that this new mechanism might overcome some of the obstacles that have limited the effectiveness of UN actions.

This suggests a common paradox in humanitarian assistance: those most in need of aid tend to be found in the areas most difficult for international organizations to access. Nowhere is this more evident than in Syria's "hard-to-reach" areas and "besieged communities." According to OCHA, the UN was able to reach less than 1 percent of the 422,000 people living in besieged areas and only 5.2 percent of the 4.8 million people in need in hard-to-reach areas.[82]

Besieged Areas

As of September 2015 an estimated 4.8 million Syrians lived in UN-designated hard-to-reach areas, most of which are in ISIS-held territories. Of 127 hard-to-reach areas, UN agencies and NGOs reached only 29 during July 2015.[83] Throughout the crisis, sieges have been used by the Syrian government and to a lesser extent by opposition armed groups. Although the government denies that it conducts sieges of civilian areas in Syria, its first short-term siege was imposed on Deraa city in 2011, with longer-term sieges then used in rural Damascus in 2012 with an intensification of sieges in 2013. In August 2015 UN secretary-general

Ban Ki-moon estimated that 422,000 people lived in areas besieged by armed groups, including 163,500 besieged by government forces in Eastern Ghouta; 4,000 by government forces in Daarayya; 266,500 by non-state armed groups in Zahra and Nabul; and 228,000 by ISIS in the government-controlled western neighborhoods of Deir-ez-Zor city.[84] The Syrian-American Medical Society argued that the numbers were far higher and, if partially besieged communities are taken into account, the figure as of early 2015 was probably over 1 million people.[85]

As the Independent International Commission of Inquiry on the Syrian Arab Republic observed, "Siege warfare is conducted in a ruthlessly coordinated and planned manner, aimed at forcing a population, collectively, to surrender or suffer starvation." Government forces continue to besiege rebel-controlled districts in eastern and southern Damascus. "Civilian residents in these areas have died from starvation, from injuries sustained in aerial bombardments and, as a consequence, from a lack of medical care." It is not only the government that has used sieges, but also other anti-government armed groups, particularly ISIS. "Wherever sieges are employed, a black market economy has been created for goods that are smuggled in or are ushered through checkpoints through payment of bribes." Sieges are also a business. "In most instances, armed actors remain able to function. It is the civilian population who suffers."[86]

Areas under siege, such as Aleppo and Homs, have little or no access to aid. Indeed, both the government of Syria and opposition groups have cut off movement to and from certain areas for years.[87] UN Security Council resolutions 2139 and 2165 demanded that all parties to the conflict, and in particular the Syrian authorities, end all attacks against civilians, lift all sieges, and provide unfettered cross-line and cross-border humanitarian aid. According to Amnesty International, "well over a year after the resolutions were passed, the parties to the conflict continue to violate them, and international law, with impunity."[88]

Counting besieged areas is a tricky and difficult task, particularly in the absence of traditional human rights monitoring mechanisms. The Syrian-American Medical Society not only came up with a different estimate of the number of people living in besieged areas but questioned the methodology employed by OCHA to designate these areas, adding a classification of "partially-besieged,'" which somewhat overlaps with OCHA's classification of hard-to-reach areas. The author of that report noted that OCHA may underestimate the scale of the problem because of a reluctance to antagonize the government and its desire to be able to continue operating in Syria.

Amnesty International in August 2015 estimated that more than 400,000 civilians lived in areas under siege.[89] It studied the situation for the 163,0000 people living under siege in Eastern Ghouta, an industrial and agricultural area thirteen kilometers northeast of Damascus, where chemical weapons were used in 2013. Parts of the area have been under siege by the Syrian government since late 2012. The report found that "the Syrian government is systematically subjecting civilians in Eastern Ghouta to an unlawful siege which restricts civilians, the wounded and sick from being able to leave the area and restricts the delivery of humanitarian and medical assistance and goods needed for survival, as well as striking medics, aid workers and facilities in indiscriminate attacks."

Non-state armed groups, according to Amnesty International, are also responsible for inflating the price of food, arbitrarily restricting the movement of civilians wishing to leave, and abducting and arbitrarily detaining people. "According to the Syrian American Medical Society, 208 civilians died from the lack of food or access to medical care in Eastern Ghouta from 21 October 2012 to 31 January 2015," the report said. This is an area where protests began in Douma in March 2011. By early 2013 much of Eastern Ghouta had fallen under the de facto control of an array of some sixteen armed groups opposed to the Syrian government. In April 2013 the Syrian army mounted an offensive against the armed groups and tightened restrictions on civilians. Amnesty estimated that 9,000 fighters were in Eastern Ghouta and said fighting had seen each side take the offensive at different times.[90]

As a forthcoming Mercy Corps report makes clear, the impact of sieges varies, depending on whether they occur in a rural or urban area. Sieges of urban areas typically involve a more thorough blockade and greater hardship than in rural areas because urban populations are unable to supplement their food with agriculture. The research also finds that prices of basic foodstuffs and other necessities are often manipulated by different parties to the conflict. Internal armed groups control market prices to raise profits while armed groups sometimes deliberately manipulate internal markets to reduce local farmers' profits by allowing in convoys of certain goods at strategic points in time.

In July 2015 medical assistance reached just 1.8 percent of the population considered by the UN to be besieged, and no food or other types of humanitarian relief could be provided. This figure was even lower than the previous month, when 5 percent of those in officially recognized besieged areas were reached with medical aid, but no other assistance of any kind.[91] It may be, however, that local organizations and international nongovernmental organizations operating covertly were able to assist some people in these areas and their contributions are simply not registered by the UN system.

Conditions for those living in besieged areas are unbeliev-ably difficult, with extreme levels of unemployment leading to desperation and poverty; limited food, water, and fuel sup-plies; and escalating food prices.[92] The Syrian American Med-ical Society cited the cost of a kilo of sugar in Damascus city at $0.66, while in Eastern Ghouta during the 2013–14 siege it reached $19.00 (and dropped to $3.30 after March 2014).[93]

How do civilians survive such conditions? Reports are that they use firewood for fuel, grow rooftop gardens, move field hospitals underground, scavenge, and resort to boiling weeds, extracting glue from shoes, and eating cats and dogs. Some civilians starve to death.

Cross-Border Operations

Cross-border operations to provide aid to displaced and other vulnerable Syrians living in areas outside the control of the Syrian government have been going on almost since the beginning of the conflict. These operations have pro-vided life-saving assistance to hundreds of thousands, per-haps millions, of vulnerable Syrians. And yet, because these operations are opposed by the Syrian government, aid orga-nizations and other actors have largely operated under the radar in areas controlled by a wide range of armed groups, some of whom have seen the provision of relief assistance as a means of consolidating their positions.

In July 2014 the UN Security Council authorized cross-border aid delivery without the consent of the Syrian govern-ment at four border crossings in Jordan, Iraq, and Turkey.[94] The final text of the council's resolution was itself a compro-mise, as proponents of these operations had wanted permission to use all available border crossings. In December 2014 the UN announced that the Security Council had renewed until January 2016 the authorization for UN agencies and partners to deliver cross-border aid via two border crossings in Turkey (as well as one in Iraq and one in Jordan). The UN announced in January 2015 that forty aid shipments to Syria had been made via Turkey (and another fourteen from Jordan) since the Security Council first authorized the cross-border routes in July 2014.[95] The UN reported that a total of 600,000 Syrians had been assisted over the previous six months with food, water, and medical supplies. However, in March 2015 a coalition of NGOs, including the Norwegian Refugee Council and Oxfam, said the resolutions on cross-border aid had not been translated into action on the ground. In fact, the agencies said, the number of Syrians in need of assistance in hard-to-reach areas had almost doubled to 4.8 million.[96]

In spite of UN efforts and reports on aid shipments, UN involvement in cross-border aid operations has been minimal in comparison with aid operations by other international actors, including donor governments, international NGOs, Syrian diaspora groups, Turkish and Gulf NGOs, and a number of other actors. The fact that such operations are taking place outside of traditional coordination mechanisms means that there has been a lack of transparency about the operations and especially about what happens to the aid when it is delivered inside Syria. Virtually all international actors involved with these cross-border aid deliveries rely on Syrian partners to distribute the aid, including Syrian civil society organizations, local councils, and perhaps armed groups.

There have been persistent reports of aid being used to support military operations of opposition armed groups.

A December 2014 *New Yorker* article noted that ISIS was widely believed to have established a presence in Gaziantep, the main hub for cross-border aid operations in southern Turkey.[97] Americans in Gaziantep were warned that ISIS operatives were tracking their activities. U.S. aid for local councils had been going to rebel-held areas of four northern Syrian provinces: Raqqa, Deir-ez-Zor, Aleppo, and Idlib. But by summer 2014, ISIS had seized much of Raqqa and Deir-ez-Zor. According to the *New Yorker*'s sources, this sparked a debate in Washington about whether the cross-border aid was enabling ISIS, but the aid continued to flow in. There is also a debate about the accountability of aid administered from Gaziantep. Despite the U.S. use of remote monitoring techniques such as GPS devices, along with photos, signed receipts, and reports from third parties, one Syrian opposition spokesman overseeing cross-border aid estimated that 30–40 percent was lost to scams by warlords and others. By June 2015, shortly after its victory in Palmyra, ISIS had reportedly captured an area of Aleppo province that gave it access to the road to the Bab al-Salam border crossing, threatening a major aid supply route.[98]

According to OCHA, as of July 2015 seven UN agencies and the International Organization for Migration had deployed 2,463 trucks worth of assistance in 104 consignments, reaching around 386,000 people with food, almost 50,000 with health supplies, 10,000 with water, and 12,700 with non-food items. The U.S. government reported in September 2015 that it was reaching 5 million people per month in Syria.[99] It is difficult to interpret such figures since a person "reached" with assistance may have received a one-time food parcel sufficient for a month or a five-liter container of water or perhaps a bucket or tarp. The World Food

Program's report that it provided food to 4 million Syrians every month is more reassuring.

Currently the bulk of cross-border aid by UN agencies and their partners—forty of fifty-four shipments in 2014—originates in Turkey and reaches only the northern region of Syria, while aid moving in from Jordan tends to be distributed near the shared border in Syria's south.[100]

Local and Diaspora Groups

Almost all cross-border aid is distributed through local Syrian organizations, which are tasked with the risk of traveling inside Syria, organizing the distributions, and reporting back to donors. Using local agencies is good practice—they know the language, culture, and communities. Some of these civil society groups existed in Syria before the war, some emerged in response to the crisis, and other groups were formed in diaspora communities that wanted desperately to help. "In Syria, the local groups that are now doing so much of the lifesaving aid are in many places the only ones with real access to desperate Syrians who cannot survive without help," two researchers for Refugees International reported in May 2015.[101] But staff and volunteers in these organizations work in dangerous environments and their funding depends on subgrants where reporting processes can be onerous. There are tensions between donors and these local groups, with complaints that the methods being used may be appropriate for non-conflict areas but are impractical in the active conflict zones inside Syria. Some changes have been made in these procedures—such as documentation of aid delivery through photographs rather than signed forms, but given donors' concerns about diversion of aid and the lack of capacity by the Syrian organizations, these tensions are likely to continue.[102] Training of Syrian organizations has taken place on specific issues—such as how to track and record financial transactions, on international humanitarian law, and on how to address the special needs of women and children in programming. But the Refugees International mission found that follow-up to these training activities had been inadequate, and the researchers called for more concerted work on capacity building.[103]

The money trail is complicated. A donor government—say the United States or the United Kingdom—gives funds to UN agencies and to international nongovernmental organizations (who also receive other funds from the UN), which in turn pass the money on to Syrian diaspora groups, which in turn give the aid to local groups inside Syria, which then give actual aid to people in need.[104] Some diaspora groups have been able to meet U.S. government eligibility requirements for humanitarian response funding and can directly apply for grants from the U.S. government.[105] There are also indications that coordination mechanisms have improved their responsiveness to concerns of local agencies by including them in coordination mechanisms and providing interpretation.[106]

SAFE HAVENS, NO-FLY ZONES, AND OTHER FORMS OF INTERVENTION

As mentioned in the preceding chapter, Turkey has been at the forefront of calling for the establishment of a safe zone inside Syria. Although the issue has not gained widespread traction (and even less so in light of the recent Russian involvement in the conflict), it is a suggestion that continues to surface in different quarters—and perhaps for different reasons. Important questions arise about exactly what constitutes a safe zone, although there seems to be a consensus that some degree of military force would be required to maintain it. Is a safe zone a weapons-free, neutral area administered by humanitarian actors to protect civilians? Or is it an area where opposition forces can move freely and where military personnel are responsible not only for protecting civilians seeking safety there but also for distributing humanitarian relief? Will creation of the safe zone be negotiated by humanitarian actors or imposed by force? If the latter, what level of military force will be required to guarantee the safety of the civilians taking refuge there, and who will provide that military force?

Some of the strongest calls for safe zones have come from actors with little or no operational humanitarian experience. In effect, these calls seem to represent a form of "intervention lite"—less costly and risky than outright military intervention to stop the carnage but seemingly more robust than merely providing aid.[107]

The historical record of safe zones as tools for protecting civilians is a decidedly mixed one, with the mass killings in Srebrenica, Bosnia, in 1995 standing out as the starkest example of their failure. Taylor Seyboldt, in his classic analysis of different forms of humanitarian intervention, found that those with specific and limited objectives tend to be most successful.[108] Phil Orchard looked at the failed interventions in Somalia (1991–95) and Bosnia (1991–95) and found that safe areas in the 1990s all suffered from three problems. First, safe areas were intended to meet an incompatible combination of objectives, namely supporting civilian protection and humanitarian assistance while seeking to contain potential refugee flows in their home state. Second, the safe areas that failed were based on a flawed logic—either relying on, at best, grudging consent of the affected state or bellig-

erent parties or on appeals to respect the legitimacy of the
UN Security Council. Third, the creators of safe areas failed
to take into account the response of belligerents, who often
directly targeted civilians and had no stake in the intervention to protect them.[109]

One fairly successful use of a safe haven occurred in 1991
in northern Iraq when some 500,000 Iraqi Kurds sought to
escape the brutality of Saddam Hussein's regime by fleeing into Turkey. The Turkish government refused to admit
them and instead prevailed upon the international community to create and police a safe zone inside northern Iraq,
called Operation Provide Comfort. With a "no-fly zone"
enforced by U.S., British, and French aircraft, this safe area
functioned more or less well, and the displaced Iraqi Kurds
were able to return to their communities within months.
This experience has undoubtedly influenced Turkey's calls
for a safe zone in Syria. But the Iraqi government was forced
to acquiesce to the creation of the Kurdish zone, while the
Assad regime remains steadfastly opposed to incursions of
its sovereignty—and therein lies the rub.

Under Chapter VII of the UN Charter, when the UN
Security Council determines that there is a threat to international peace and security, it can take measures deemed
necessary to restore peace and security. "Such measures
may include the imposition of safe areas to secure an endan-
gered population, even without the consent of the parties
to a conflict. Subsequent UN resolutions have upheld these
rules and created UN-facilitated safe areas, such as UNSC
Resolution 819, which established "safe areas" in Bosnia and
Herzegovina during the war in the 1990s. As a practical
matter, the creation of a safe zone—absent consent of the
parties—will usually require some element of force to deter
attacks and protect those inside the zone."[110]

A recent workshop jointly organized by the International Committee for the Red Cross and InterAction articulated a number of concerns about safe zones. For example, they may act as a pull factor for refugees, as seems to be occurring at the present time in South Sudan. A report on the workshop said: "The establishment of a safe area near an international boundary could result in a tightening of borders by neighboring states. Such border restrictions may lead to *refoulement*, and undermine security for civilians that are unable to reach a safe area or flee to a safe refuge outside their country. Declaring a safe area could also create the illusion of security for civilians, and may result in their taking risks they would not otherwise take, including returning to their country of origin in adverse conditions."[111] Establishing such an area could blur the lines between military objectives and humanitarian goals and compromise the rights of people seeking asylum, the Red Cross/InterAction report said. A safe area or buffer zone established without the consent of the state could "be perceived as a target, posing new risks for civilians seeking safety and could also become a magnet for armed opposition groups."[112]

No-fly zones also were discussed in the context of NATO's intervention in Libya in 2011—an intervention cited since by both proponents and opponents of no-fly zones. The Red Cross/InterAction report noted: "A no-fly zone imposed by one or more states on another state (without consent) may violate state sovereignty, and initiate an international armed conflict." Establishing such a zone, the report added, could "entail significant offensive operations against the forces posing a threat to civilians, at least temporarily, leading to serious consequences for the civilian population concerned." Establishing a buffer zone would require ground forces to secure arms caches and clear out belligerents with weapons. Air operations alone may not be adequate to prevent or mitigate violence on the ground and instead could speed up violence on the ground. Finally, the report said, "military interventions that have the declared objective of protecting civilians run the risk of morphing into operations to defeat an enemy rather than intervening impartially on behalf of a civilian population at risk." [113]

While there are powerful arguments that safe zones may not provide protection to Syrian civilians (and could, in fact, put them in increased danger), the almost total lack of other options for protecting Syrians (and stemming the refugee flow) has led thoughtful observers to argue that such safe areas could be a "less bad" option than the current dismal situation. The result has been a robust public debate about whether, how, where, and in what form a safe zone could be established. [114]

It is quite striking that humanitarians—who were at the forefront of calling for intervention in Rwanda and Somalia two decades ago—have been almost silent on the issue of safe zones for Syria. As one senior official of a humanitarian organization remarked: "We've been there. We've seen it doesn't work." Diane Paul is one of the few experienced humanitarian workers who has called for the establishment of a safe zone, albeit with a set of conditions that likely would be impossible to implement. [115] The idea is also advocated by a former ISIS hostage. [116] Writing from a different perspective, Michael O'Hanlon argues that such a zone could not only protect civilians but also support the moderate opposition, which is perhaps the best hope of bringing an end to the bloodbath—itself a humanitarian objective. [117] Phil Gordon, James Dobbins, and Jeff Martini argue that establishing three safe zones, as part of a negotiated cease-fire, could set the stage for a longer-term transitional arrangement. [118]

On the political front, Turkey has been one of the strongest and earliest champions of a safe zone in Syria, perhaps seeing it as a way of decreasing the number of refugees arriving on its borders—or perhaps recalling the largely positive experience of the 1991 safe zone established to protect Iraqi Kurds fleeing chemical and other attacks. So far, there has been strong opposition from both Russia and China, as well as Syria. This opposition stems in part from NATO's operations in Libya in 2011, which were justified in terms of protecting civilians but which morphed into regime change. Syria rejects the notion of safe zones as violation of Syrian sovereignty or as a conspiratorial attempt to occupy and partition the country. Russia and China, which traditionally oppose UN and other interventions within national borders, maintain that safe areas would be a threat to Syria's sovereignty and territorial integrity. France and the United Kingdom have been hesitant to endorse safe areas in Syria, reportedly because of their concern with the complexity and long-term political implications of such actions.

Thus far, the U.S. government has opposed setting up safe areas in Syria, although it has indicated a willingness to at least consider the issue as part of the negotiations with Turkey to enable the United States to use the NATO air base in Incirlik for its air campaign against ISIS. Initially, the Turkish government was reluctant to cooperate unless Washington agreed to carve out a buffer zone in northern Syria.[119] Members of the U.S. Congress have been much more vocal than the White House in calling for safe areas, in particular Senator John McCain, who stated in 2012 that safe areas could be platforms for increased humanitarian aid and also staging areas for armed moderate opposition groups.[120] Since then former secretary of state

Hillary Rodham Clinton and some Republican presidential candidates have also advocated some type of no-fly zone in Syria.[121]

Russian military intervention in support of the Syrian regime seems to have put a damper on discussions of safe zones in Syria, at least for the time being.[122] Russian airstrikes, beginning in September 2015, disrupted aid operations, destroyed medical facilities, and caused hundreds of civilian deaths.[123] In November 2015 Russian jets struck areas near IDP camps inside Syria near the Turkish border, killing at least fifty people, followed shortly afterwards by the Turkish downing of a Russian jet.[124] The crisis that erupted in Russian-Turkish relations after this attack made the idea of a "no-fly zone," let alone a safe zone, pretty much moot. Russia has not only imposed economic sanctions on Turkey but has also moved ballistic missiles into Syria to deter any Turkish planes from entering Syrian airspace.[125] Furthermore, Russian president Vladimir Putin, in his address to the nation in December 2015, made it quite clear that Turkish jets or military entering Syria would be prime targets.[126] This in effect created a de facto no-fly zone, albeit with an entirely different motivation than discussed in Western circles.[127]

Although the current political situation precludes serious discussions of safe areas or a no-fly zone, it is likely that the political context will change again in the coming months, and considerations of such alternatives could once again be on the table.

While proposals for a safe area or a no-fly zone are problematic on many levels, the fact remains that there are no easy solutions for protecting Syria's civilians from the ravages of an increasingly convoluted and brutal war. Displacement is, above all, a protection strategy for individuals and families. Fleeing their communities in search of safety is sometimes the only way to survive. As long as the war continues, Syrians will continue to be displaced. And as long as the international community is unable to come up with a means of resolving this terrible conflict, outsiders will be forced to search for ways to mitigate the harm to those suffering the effects of war.

We turn now to exploring some of the challenges that Syria's displacement poses to the international system.

CHAPTER 4

Syrian Displacement and the International Order

Syria's war was not caused by the international community but rather was the product of deep-seated political and economic factors endemic to the region and specific actions taken by the Bashar al-Assad regime and various insurgent groups. While the war has been abetted by international actors who have supplied arms and fighters to all sides of the conflict, it is important to underscore that the roots of the conflict are mostly internal. Similarly, the displacement of one-half of Syria's population was not caused by the international community.

But as the war and the resulting displacement pose a threat to international peace and security—the very kind of threat that systems of global governance are intended to address—we look now at what Syrian displacement tells us about the present international order. This chapter begins with a synthesis of central themes emerging from this study, followed by recommendations for moving forward. In particular we argue that the time is right to develop what we call a New Global Approach for Syria.

IMPLICATIONS OF SYRIAN DISPLACEMENT
FOR INTERNATIONAL ORDER

The Syrian conflict and resulting displacement are clear signs that the present international system for preventing and resolving conflicts has been deeply challenged. The United Nations was created to "save succeeding generations from the scourge of war," and the Security Council in particular was given the responsibility of ensuring global peace and security.[1] The "Responsibility to Protect" doctrine, launched with such optimism a decade ago, has utterly failed in the case of Syria. Of course, there have been other cases where the UN has successfully intervened to prevent and resolve conflicts, such as in Côte d'Ivoire, Chad, and Mali, and in cases such as South Sudan where UN peacekeeping operations have demonstrated flexibility in protecting civilians in new ways.

But robust action to halt the violence in Syria has not occurred, due to the lack of consensus among major powers about the way forward. The UN Security Council has issued resolutions calling for an end to the conflict, for the protection of civilians, and for an end to sieges of entire communities, but these resolutions have had little or no impact on the conflict on the ground. The adoption of a roadmap for peace in Syria in December 2015, calling for UN-led negotiations on a political transition and for an immediate cease-fire, offered a glimmer of hope for the way forward.[2] The political obstacles to the implementation of this long-delayed proposal are manifold.

It may be that the Syrian conflict has become too complex, the political interests too diverse, and the proliferation of actors too great for the UN to be able to take effective action to prevent chaos. These factors suggest that the international community should tackle the much-discussed need for Security Council reform. We do not have the expertise to propose such changes, and there are many proposals by much more knowledgeable groups about what is needed.[3] But we can say on the basis of this study that the present international system for preventing the war and resolving the underlying conflict that has displaced so many has—for five years—failed in Syria.

In spite of growing attention to the role of regional organizations, Syrian displacement is also a clear indictment of the failure of regional bodies to prevent and resolve crises. While both the Arab League and the Organization of Islamic Cooperation suspended Syria's membership in 2011 and 2012, respectively, neither has played a significant role in addressing the conflict. The Arab League, which played an important role in supporting the use of military force in Libya (from which it later backtracked), has been almost completely absent on the Syria conflict. The Organization of Islamic Cooperation has failed to bring about a unified position on the Syrian crisis among its members. The principal actions of both the Arab League and the Islamic organization have been to call on the UN Security Council to take action.[4] In failing to rise above specific political interests, regional actors in the Middle East have not provided an alternative conflict resolution strategy for Syria. Thus far, they also have failed to offer a coherent regional approach to the refugee situation, even though some of their members are the most directly impacted by the crisis.

The European Union has been active on Syria, but its actions also have failed to bring about either an end to the conflict or even a coordinated approach to the refugee crisis. EU engagement in support of UN-led efforts to bring about a political solution has been more robust than those of either the Arab League or the Organization of Islamic Cooperation, but in the end, the EU has adopted the same approach: calling on the UN to resolve the conflict. This seems to indicate that the role of regional organizations is limited in conflict resolution; the tools available to them are simply inadequate to bring an end to Syria's civil war.

However, the lack of European solidarity in responding to the initial Mediterranean migration crisis in 2013–14 and to the much larger mass influx by sea and land in 2015 raises fundamental questions about the future of European integration. Rather than rising to the challenge of creating a stronger union through a common approach to the crisis, the policies adopted can best be described as a "beggar thy neighbor" approach. The impact on European unity of the refugees from Syria, Afghanistan, Iraq, and elsewhere— coupled with the aftermath of the November 2015 terrorist attacks in Paris—could be profound, threatening the tremendous progress made to enable free movement across European borders, including the Schengen agreement.[5] The imposition of border controls within Europe, on more than a temporary basis, could have long-term consequences in ways that call into question the very principles of European unity.[6]

The solution to the crisis of Syrian refugees and internally displaced people (IDPs) is political. It has long been a mantra in the humanitarian community that "there are no humanitarian solutions to humanitarian crises." The solutions have to be political, in which different groups in a society somehow find a way to settle their differences. This is particularly apparent in Syria. Former secretary of state

Madeleine Albright rightly noted that the crisis in Syria "is not only a humanitarian emergency, but also a political emergency. It is a series of political failures that have led to the grave situation that we find today."[7] No matter how much money is mobilized for humanitarian aid, or how many humanitarian workers are deployed, or how many refugees are resettled, Syria's humanitarian crisis will persist until the conflict is resolved and possibly beyond it, too.

Displacement—whether cross-border or internally—always has political consequences. But the refugee/security nexus has catapulted to global attention in the case of Syrian refugees, particularly after the Paris attacks. Even before then there was a perception in Jordan, Turkey, and Lebanon that crime was increasing because of the presence of Syrian refugees, although there was little, if any, hard evidence for that conclusion. Since the November 2015 Paris attacks, the association of Syrian refugees with terrorism has taken on a particularly ugly tone, especially in the United States. A paradigm shift in understanding the relationship between refugees and security is urgently needed, based on solid empirical evidence and an acknowledgement of the security risks that may result from protracted displacement. As displacement drags on, and if solutions do not emerge, it is possible, in the words of one expert, that refugees "will become involved in political violence and be susceptible to militant recruitment . . . protracted situations result in reduced expectations for the future, increasing feelings of hopelessness, and desperation among refugees/displaced persons."[8] Hence, mobilizing the political will to ensure decent protection for the refugees and respond to their needs, including offering them the possibility to rebuild their lives and take control of their futures, will be critical.

Thus far, resettlement of Syrian refugees has played a

very minor role in the response to the massive Syrian displacement crisis. Resettlement, unlike asylum, is based on a process of identifying, selecting, vetting, and supporting refugees from countries of first refuge to third countries outside the region. As a system developed in the aftermath of World War II and particularly during the Cold War era, resettlement has become a tool for protecting refugees who face risks where they are and for finding solutions for particularly vulnerable refugees. It is also a bureaucratic, slow, and expensive process, costing an average of some $15,000 per resettled refugee. [9] And yet, resettlement is a strong example of a truly durable solution. Resettled refugees do very well, and they contribute to their host countries. This is particularly the case in the United States, which has a long tradition of refugee resettlement and which played a leadership role in developing the global resettlement system.[10] In the present political context, it will require considerable political leadership and effort both in the EU and the United States to advocate for and implement a policy of resettling Syrian refugees. Yet, without a robust resettlement program, it will be difficult to strengthen the principle of burden sharing, which is in urgent need of reaffirmation, along with the very values that the transatlantic community is supposed to represent.

Responding to displacement inside Syria is a far more complex and politically treacherous endeavor than responding to more than 4.5 million refugees in many different countries. The international community has provided massive support for assistance inside Syria, and many dedicated local and international staff have risked their lives to deliver relief. In spite of these efforts, assistance to displaced people still inside Syria—as well as to those who are trapped in their communities—is insufficient. It took years for the UN

Security Council to adopt decisions enabling international
agencies to be able to provide some assistance across borders
and in areas not controlled by the Syrian government. The
relatively "soft law" on aiding IDPs has been as ineffective as
the more formal "hard law" on the protection of civilians in
combat zones. The disregard of these laws by state actors has
been exacerbated by the practices of non-state actors that
often have deliberately used civilians as shields or targets. In
other situations of internal displacement, working to build
capacity and political will of the government is the obvious
approach, but this does not seem to be possible in Syria

As discussed in chapter 3, the notions of "safe areas,"
"no-fly zones," and "humanitarian corridors" are frequently
brought up as means to protect both IDPs and civilians generally inside Syria. These proposals need to be approached
very carefully. "Safe havens" have also been advocated as
areas that could eventually evolve into mini-states consti-
tuting the basis of a confederal Syria.[11] They could also play
a role if a completely different constellation of states emerges
in the aftermath of the conflict—consisting of ethnically
and religious homogenous stand-alone stages, including one
"Sunnistan."[12] But as of now, there is a striking lack of political consensus on whether and how such safe zones might
function.

THE INTERRELATIONSHIP BETWEEN SOLUTIONS
TO THE CONFLICT AND DISPLACEMENT

Any solution to the Syrian conflict must take displacement
into account. If Assad remains in power, the possibilities of
large-scale refugee returns are limited. It is hard to overestimate the bitterness and alienation felt by many refugees
at the suffering caused by the Assad regime. Studies show

that peace processes that fail to take into account the desires of the displaced populations are not sustainable.[13] The Security Council in its resolutions has a tendency to mention displacement only in terms of returns of refugees.[14] This is both simplistic and inadequate. In the case of Syrian refugees, it is unlikely that most will return home in the foreseeable future, but if and when they do return, they will need robust support to reintegrate into their home communities. Alternative solutions—such as local integration and resettlement—should be considered in any peace agreement.

Offering opportunities to refugees to develop their own livelihoods would not just benefit the economies of host communities but also improve the capacity of refugees to return home when the possibility emerges. The World Bank, in a 2015 report on Syrian refugees in Turkey, advocated taking a more developmental approach to supplement the humanitarian response and argued that "experience shows that when refugees are supported in becoming socially and economically self-reliant, and given freedom of movement and protection, they are more likely to contribute to their host country. They are also more likely to be able to undertake a successful return process."[15] Supporting the "integration" of refugees into their host communities especially through access to livelihood opportunities does not necessarily mean fewer returns.[16]

Any solution to the Syrian conflict needs to provide sufficient funds for the physical reconstruction of the country. This will be a daunting task. As a former Syrian official noted, "if or when the war ends, any government will find itself ruling over a pile of rubble." The cost of rebuilding some 2.1 million homes, one-half the country's hospitals, and more than 7,000 schools destroyed in Syria is put at more than $300 billion by this official, who also said: "I don't know who will fund this."[17] As much as it may seem unrealistic at this point, the international community needs to start thinking about a Middle East Recovery Plan, somewhat reminiscent of the Marshall Plan to rebuild Europe after World War II. If the Vienna process and the UN roadmap for peace in Syria do indeed take hold and progress is made toward a political solution in Syria, this idea of a "recovery plan" that also addresses the return of refugees and IDPs is essential. Such an initiative could grow out of a comprehensive regional approach to the Syrian refugee crisis as discussed later here.

Any solution to the Syrian conflict also must provide an accounting for the crimes committed. Transitional justice mechanisms are painfully slow and rarely address displacement.[18] This must change in any post-conflict plan for Syria. Whether criminal prosecutions through the International Criminal Court, or truth commissions, or justice-sensitive security sector reform—use of these transitional justice mechanisms could play a central role in determining whether the displaced can return and whether a post-conflict Syria will be stable and secure.[19] There is a very real danger that a quick fix (though even quick fixes seem distant at the time of this writing) will contain the seeds of the next conflict. If there are large-scale retributions, if the rule of law cannot be ensured, if those responsible for dropping barrel bombs remain in power, then further conflict and displacement are likely.

To cite again the Independent International Commission of Inquiry on the Syrian Arab Republic:

> Government forces have committed gross violations of human rights and the war crimes of murder, torture, rape, sexual violence and targeting civilians. Government forces disregarded the special protec-

tion accorded to hospitals and medical personnel. . . . Anti-Government armed groups have committed the war crimes of murder, execution without due process, torture, hostage-taking and attacking protected objects. . . . The litany of abuses listed here captures only part of the trauma experienced by Syrian civilians, as the world stands witness.[20]

Syrian displacement is inextricably linked with these larger questions of accountability and governance processes. But displacement also raises specific challenges to how the world responds to major humanitarian emergencies. In this regard, we offer reflections from two very different perspectives: bottom up and top down. The top-down approach is more comfortable for those working on either the national or international level as well as for academics; somehow it is easier to figure out the elements of a grand plan for refugees (and we present some of these ideas below) than to enter the messy world of trying to understand how refugees and IDPs support themselves without international assistance. Nonetheless, we suggest that understanding the bottom-up approach may in fact turn out to be the best hope for refugees and IDPs.

RECOGNIZING REFUGEES AS ACTORS

While refugees and IDPs are usually depicted in Western media only as the victims of conflict, they are survivors. Displacement is, first and foremost, a protection strategy. While national authorities and international agencies have a responsibility to protect and assist them, the fact is that most are surviving not because of international aid but by their own means. And it is likely that most will find their own solutions without international support; certainly that has been the case in the resolution of most displacement situations. As with the case of Syrian refugees today, local integration was rejected by all the governments hosting Iraqi refugees in the mid-2000s. And yet, Dawn Chatty and Nisrine Mansour found that while integration wasn't possible, local "accommodation" is taking place where Iraqis are blending in with their host communities (including through intermarriage with locals), and few are deported.[21] Similarly, Katy Long found that mobility is an effective protection strategy for refugees; in fact, large numbers of Central American refugees in the 1990s found their solutions through migration rather than through formal international schemes.[22]

These findings suggest two implications for international actors. First, they should be more humble in considering the effects of their actions. Second, more concerted and sustained international efforts are needed to help refugees and IDPs to survive and to find their own solutions. Refugees in neighboring countries are running out of resources, and their coping strategies are under tremendous strain. For many, savings have been depleted and cuts in international assistance mean that minimum basic needs are not being met. The fact that so many Syrians have made the painful decision to move further away from Syria and to make risky journeys to Europe is a sign that their resilience is wearing thin. International humanitarian agencies are simply unable to meet the assistance needs of the refugees, and they often cannot protect refugees and displaced persons even in areas where they are working. [23]

In the case of refugees living in neighboring host countries, the single biggest change that would allow them to prosper would be having the right to legal employment and access to livelihoods. The governments of the region have

legitimate reasons for not wanting refugees to work, including concerns about domestic unemployment and potential
political backlash. But if the refugees are to remain in these
countries for at least some period of time, their ability to
work would both reduce their burden on the finances of host
countries and their dependence on international assistance.
Having jobs would allow them the dignity that comes with
self-sufficiency, as well as enable them to contribute to the
economy of host communities. The question then becomes:
How can the international community support the host
governments in such a way that they see a benefit in allowing refugees access to employment?

This is a tough issue that flies in the face of the current
"incentive structure" in which host governments receive
international funds for care and maintenance of refugees.
There is a need for a new incentive structure for incorporat-
ing refugees into local labor markets and enabling them to
access a livelihood. It is encouraging that this idea was incorporated into the G-20 leaders' November 2015 communiqué in the form of a call for "efforts to ensure that refugees
can access . . . livelihood opportunities."[24] If the incentive
structure were changed so that host governments realized
a direct benefit from allowing refugees to work (with appropriate safeguards for those unable to work), this would
have an enormous effect on refugees' ability both to survive
in the current climate and to move toward solutions. Such
a change would not have to happen either immediately or
across the board. For example, there may be ways of grad-
ually opening up the labor market to refugees by starting
with specific sectors, such as allowing Syrian school teachers to be paid for teaching Syrian refugee children.

The issue of livelihoods is also tied closely to education.
Too many Syrian refugee children are out of school because

they need to work to support their families. It is widely rec-ognized that they are not in school and are at risk of be-coming a "lost generation" with consequent implications for security. Livelihoods and education need to be approached in a holistic fashion and, beyond security considerations, their impact on economic growth needs to be well under-stood. While ensuring access to education to all refugee children will require additional funds, other steps need to be taken, including supporting efforts by universities in host countries to admit Syrian refugees and finding ways to cer-tify refugee students' academic records when documents are missing. Discussions of refugee education usually focus on primary schools, but opportunities for providing university and vocational training for older students could well be key to Syria's near-term future.

Providing education and livelihood opportunities to ref-ugees has significant financial, social, and political conse-quences for the governments hosting Syrian refugees. These consequences need to be taken seriously by the international community.

It is important to underscore that the burden of protect-ing and assisting refugees has largely fallen on the shoulders of major host countries—primarily Jordan, Lebanon, and Turkey. As this study has detailed, the governments of these three countries have been on the front line of responding to refugees. While this study has been critical of some as-pects of their response, they have done amazing work with inadequate international support. The international refugee system, created in the aftermath of World War II, was built on the premise that responsibility for refugees is an interna-tional responsibility, not just the responsibility of the gov-ernments of the countries to which refugees happened to arrive.[25] The implicit "deal" was that if a government kept its borders open and allowed refugees to arrive, the international community would play its part. In the case of Syria, international donors have provided an unprecedented influx of funds—far more per capita than for refugees displaced by other conflicts that are not in the media spotlight. Still, the support has not been enough: not enough to provide lives of dignity for the refugees, and not enough to reassure the host governments. In other situations (notably Southeast Asia), the resettlement of refugees relieved sufficient pressure on host governments to allow them to continue offering asylum to refugees in their countries. But resettlement opportunities for Syrians have been limited. International agencies and humanitarian actors have had to do their best with very limited and constantly diminishing funds.

Appeals by host governments and the UN system for more assistance received scant attention—until large numbers of Syrians began to arrive in Europe. Public empathy and solidarity with Syrian refugees and the accompanying positive climate in support of resettlement and assistance, however, was cut short by the Paris attacks. The resettlement issue very quickly became securitized, and in a disappointing but unsurprising manner many politicians in the United States as well as in Europe adopted xenophobic rhetoric toward Syrian refugees. Nevertheless, the governments of Canada, Germany, Sweden, and the United States, among others, continued to adhere to their commitment to receive refugees in spite of the unfavorable domestic context. But even if the number of resettlement places was to increase significantly, there are limits to resettlement, particularly if funding for increased resettlement of Syrian refugees comes at the expense of financial support for refugees in the region. In addition, the majority of the refugees likely will want to return to their homes once a settlement can be reached in

Syria and rebuild their country, even though prospects for return will decrease with time. Large-scale resettlement could undermine these efforts and could deprive post-conflict Syria of the human capital that will be needed for the mammoth task of reconstruction. Instead, the strategic use of resettlement is needed, in which a robust and viable resettlement program gives priority to vulnerable cases and supports solutions for refugees.

In the meantime, borders are closing to Syrian refugees. Host countries are experiencing fatigue resulting in part from inadequate burden sharing. Host country officials do not miss a chance to criticize the double standards of others, especially EU countries, in calling on them to keep maintain their borders open to Syrian refugees while closing their own borders.[26] An unfortunate situation has developed in terms of Turkey's open door policy since a deal was reached between the EU and Turkey to stem the flow of Syrian and other refugees and migrants. Turkey has indeed stepped up its efforts to halt human smuggling of Syrian refugees across the Aegean Sea and has stopped an increasing number of boats while constructing a wall on part of the Syrian border.[27] Yet, at the same time, human rights organizations have reported that Syrian refugees are being detained and even forcefully returned to Syria.[28] Both the EU and Turkey have the obligation to make sure that Syrians fleeing war and destruction continue to enjoy protection and that European interests in halting migratory pressures and Turkish desires for closer EU relations do not undermine refugee protection.

There are many challenges in responding to Syrian displacement: strengthening resilience and supporting refugees and IDPs to find their own solutions; ensuring protection and security for both refugees and for host communities

alike; addressing the concerns of host governments and helping them provide livelihood and education opportunities
for refugees; mobilizing not only more international assistance but more long-term development aid, even as the war
continues; ensuring that efforts to respond to humanitarian
needs contribute to a solution to the war and do not make
things worse; and recognizing the importance of addressing
displacement in whatever political solution is eventually negotiated to end the conflict. None of these challenges can be
satisfactorily addressed on its own. Rather, what is needed is
a new international approach to Syrian refugees and IDPs:
a new agreement that in essence represents a new kind of
international "bargain" for refugee response. We call this a
"New Global Approach for Syria."

This New Global Approach for Syria would provide a
holistic and comprehensive approach to finding solutions
for the 4-plus million Syrian refugees and to developing
sound alternatives to responding to the more difficult issue
of supporting solutions for Syria's 6.5 million IDPs. The New
Global Approach for Syria could serve as a model for other
large-scale displacement situations.

RECASTING THE DEAL: A NEW GLOBAL APPROACH FOR SYRIA

Syria is the most complex and massive humanitarian emergency facing the world today. The human suffering is enormous and visible. The threats to global peace and security
are obvious. World leaders must summon the political will
to come up with solutions in a context where solutions are
not obvious. The challenge is a global one, facing countries
in different parts of the world and multilateral institutions.
If ever the world community could come together in new
ways to tackle a major humanitarian crisis, Syria would be

the case. And if a new "grand experiment" on Syrian displacement were to succeed, it might offer new possibilities for joint action in other humanitarian crises.

Negotiating a New Global Approach for Syria for Syrian refugees would be a complex undertaking in which:

■ Middle East regional organizations would be challenged to be more assertive and more successful than they have been in the past. They would have to take risks in working together and put aside major political differences to focus on humanitarian needs and the common regional good. In light of recent intraregional conflicts, this is a tall order. But it also is an opportunity for Middle Eastern organizations to develop a stronger impetus and adopt a more effective role. By demonstrating their ability to work together for a common humanitarian cause, this may serve as a confidence-building measure, leading to cooperation in other areas.

■ International humanitarian and development actors finally would have to emerge from their silos and work together in a more coherent way. This, too, is a tall order, and yet there are signs from both operational humanitarian agencies and from development actors of a new willingness to work together. Humanitarian agencies can't handle the burdens alone, particularly as displacement drags on for years. If they were to step back from being in the driver's seat in protracted situations—and if development actors stepped up to the longer-term challenge—they could concentrate on improving their emergency response. Multilateral development banks, which traditionally have kept humanitarian issues at arm's length, and which are threatened by new competitors, need a new mission. They have expertise in working with failed and fragile states. What better case to address than the needs of one-half of Syria's population?

If they can build on their expertise and contribute funds, skills, and human resources to finding solutions for Syria's displaced population, they can have the opportunity to demonstrate their continued relevance by helping resolve the most pressing crisis facing the world today.

■ Host governments would have to take the political and economic risks of opening up their labor markets to refugees and making difficult decisions to give refugees a more secure legal status than they presently have. The trade-off for taking these risks would be increased security at home and more stable financial assistance not only in support of their refugee programs but also for their own development goals.

■ Donor governments—and not just the traditional roster of mostly Western governments—would have to re-commit to the principle that the protection of refugees is indeed an international responsibility and then take con-crete actions to demonstrate their solidarity with host countries on the front line. Western governments would have to be more open to leadership and ideas coming from emerging donor countries such as China and Turkey; this is a necessary trade-off for those countries' commitment to participate in international burden sharing.

■ Governments outside of the region would need to con-sider new commitments for resettlement, and new thinking will be needed on reshaping resettlement to meet the needs of future refugee emergencies.

■ International nongovernmental organizations, which have played positive and constructive roles by supporting both refugees and IDPs, would be challenged to consider new ways of working with local nongovernmental organi-zations (NGOs) and diaspora groups that offer unique re-sources for aiding Syria's displaced but often are not at the table in coordination mechanisms. The Syrian crisis offers an opportunity to find more creative ways of overcoming the divide between international and national actors. Such a synergy would be especially useful for a comprehensive needs assessment exercise that would be critical to the New Global Approach for Syria.

None of these actors is likely to be able to take the political risks associated with these actions alone. But if all of them were to indicate a willingness to make painful choices, there is a chance that a new bargain can be struck. And while all of these actions are politically painful, they all have the potential of providing long-term payoffs. Most of all they offer the possibility of addressing the serious threat to international peace and security that the Syrian refugee situation now poses. And if this "grand experiment" works for Syria, it can serve as a precedent for common action on other burning humanitarian issues. The UN has organized a full agenda of high-level meetings in 2016 where momentum could be built around this area, including the World Humanitarian Summit and the High-Level Plenary organized by the UN secretary general on Large Movements of Refugees and Migrants in September 2016. Both of these global meetings, as well as other Syria-specific initiatives, will search for new ways of responding to Syrian refugees and other population movements.

Not Starting from Scratch

There are precedents for regional efforts to resolve protracted refugee/IDP situations. In particular, two successful examples stand out: the Comprehensive Plan of Action for Indochinese Refugees between 1988 and 1996, and the International Conference on Central American Refugees between 1987 and 1994.[29] The Indochina plan was adopted in 1989 as hundreds of thousands of Vietnamese refugees were seeking to escape by land and sea; neighboring countries, overwhelmed by the influx, were closing borders and deporting refugees. The plan, in essence, represented a new "bargain" in which large numbers of people were resettled in third countries, some refugees remained in their host countries, and some were returned to Vietnam. The Central America conference brought together governments, international actors, and civil society groups to find solutions for both refugees and IDPs in a highly charged political environment. Among other things, it represented a particularly positive experience of collaboration between development and humanitarian actors. Neither of these was an easy process, and both required substantial international commitments of time, money, and national buy-in. But by and large, the participants resolved the large displacement crises of their times through different mechanisms.

There already is a somewhat similar pattern of international meetings on Syria, mostly to mobilize funding.[30] Regional efforts have been much more limited, however, and as noted above, the Organization of Islamic Cooperation in particular has failed to adopt a proactive role in responding to the refugee challenge. According to the UNHCR "Mid-Year Trends 2015" report, six Muslim countries are among both the top ten refugee-sending countries as well as the top refugee-receiving countries.[31] With the exception of Eritrea, all of these countries are members of the Organization of Islamic Cooperation. The overwhelming majority of the Syrian refugees are from member countries, and the seat of the organization is in Saudi Arabia, which is a leading donor to the Syrian humanitarian cause. Yet, strikingly, so far that organization has failed to coordinate the efforts of its membership in addressing the Syrian refugee crisis.

In the earlier stages of the Syrian displacement crisis there was an initial effort to coordinate efforts among the major Syrian refugee–receiving countries of Jordan, Lebanon, Iraq, and Turkey together with UNHCR. The so called "Ministerial Meeting of Syria Bordering Countries" held three rounds of meetings in September 2013 and then in January and May 2014 to draw attention to the situation of Syrian refugees and coordinate calls for international burden sharing.[32] However, these meetings subsequently appear to have been discontinued. Ideally, countries bordering Syria together with the Organization of Islamic Cooperation should play a central role in the New Global Approach for Syria.

Other initiatives indicate a movement by disparate actors in different forums in the same direction. The UN's Regional Refugee and Resilience Plan embodies both a robust regional approach and a commitment to supporting resilience and increased engagement by development actors. The World Bank has adopted a New Strategy for the Middle East and North Africa, which includes as central pillars increasing the resilience of host societies to deal with refugees and IDPs and creating the conditions for long-term recovery.[33] We have already referred to the G-20 communique in November 2015. The Solutions Alliance represents a new type of partnership between affected governments and development and humanitarian actors to find solutions for displacement.[34] Numerous international nongovernmental organizations have worked on the idea of achieving better interaction between relief and developmental assistance.

This seems to be a time when many initiatives are bubbling up and different actors are reaching the same conclusion that a fundamentally new approach is needed for dealing with refugee and migration influxes. While the

Syrian situation is certainly not the only case in need of such a fresh start, it is unique in the scale of displacement, the global impact, and the apparent existence of strong political will to do things differently. If ever there was a time ripe for new and innovative action, that time is now.

What Would a New Global Approach for Syria Do?

A New Global Approach for Syria could build on the experiences of the Indochina and Central America initiatives in the 1990s by tying together a commitment to maintaining open borders to refugees in the region, increased support for resilience among refugees, development of ways to support eventual solutions for refugees, the strategic use of resettlement, and increased support for host governments—particularly in opening up livelihood opportunities to refugees. All of these are difficult and costly undertakings, but if taken collectively could be more politically palatable than if undertaken individually.

Elements of the New Global Approach for Syria

The New Global Approach for Syria could include at least six essential elements:
- Reaffirming international responsibility for refugees;
- Supporting common legal and policy approaches to Syrian refugees in the region;
- Retooling elements of resettlement policy to meet the needs;
- Engaging development actors more smoothly;
- Providing a forum for developing responses to IDPs; and
- Preparing for future recovery and reconstruction

To begin with, our suggested approach should recommit to the principle that the protection of refugees is indeed an international responsibility. However, this responsibility will need to be a truly global one and not shouldered just by traditional donor countries, most of them in the West. Emerging powers, especially Brazil, China, India, and others, will need to extend support, too. In that sense the recent G-20 summit decision to include in the communiqué a commitment to help with refugee issues around the world was a good step in the right direction. It will be important that China, as the host of the next G-20 summit, keeps this issue on the agenda and pursues efforts toward its implementation. This could also be an occasion to strengthen the 1951 Refugee Convention and UNHCR Executive Committee decisions, especially those pertaining to mass influx situations.

A New Global Approach for Syria should provide countries in the region hosting Syrian refugees with the space to develop common legal and policy approaches to those refugees. Ideally, the host governments would ratify the 1951 Refugee Convention and put refugee determination procedures in place. However, since under current circumstances this seems politically impossible and in any event would be a long-term process, the countries could at least agree on common legal approaches to forms of temporary protection, perhaps modeled on Turkey's policies. This is where a regional deal resembling the one between Turkey and the EU could provide the capacity-building means for the host countries. A regional forum could provide the opportunity to develop regional standards for treatment of refugees.[35]

Resettlement needs to be reaffirmed as a core component of refugee protection and assistance. As noted above, resettlement has played a very small role thus far in providing solutions to Syrian refugees, and it needs to be strengthened, reinvigorated, and developed into an important strategic tool as part of the New Global Approach for Syria. This will require significant rethinking—not only by UNHCR and the traditional resettlement countries but also by countries that have not yet played a role in resettling refugees.

More countries should be encouraged to offer resettlement slots, and they should be recognized for doing so. Canadian prime minister Justin Trudeau's decision to reverse the previous government's more restrictive policy and instead take an initial 25,000 Syrian refugees was a commendable development.[36] The decision by Australia to receive 12,000 Syrian refugees is also a positive development.[37] However, a much greater effort will be needed to respond to the scale of the crisis. It will be important to find ways of encouraging a wider range of countries to join the ranks of traditional resettlement countries. As of mid-December 2015, out of the thirty countries that made 125,600 places available to the UNHCR for the resettlement of Syrian refugees, only Argentina, Brazil, Belarus, and Uruguay were from outside the list of traditional resettlement countries: the United States, EU, Australia, Canada, and New Zealand.[38] Other countries—for example in Latin America, Asia, and the Persian Gulf—should be encouraged to do their part in receiving Syrian refugees for resettlement. In particular, countries such as Iran and Russia could begin to accept Syrian refugees for resettlement. Armenia, for example, has opened its doors to Syrian refugees of Armenian descent but could be encouraged and supported to receive Yazidi refugees, even if in modest numbers given the small size of the country and the economic difficulties it faces. Finally, wealthy Gulf countries, including Saudi Arabia, have not been particularly forthcoming in receiving Syrian refugees.[39] They have indeed contributed generous funds for humanitarian assistance and also host expatriate Syrian communities, but they have been reluctant to receive Syrian refugees, so far.[40] The New Global Approach for Syria might borrow a page from the climate change negotiations and suggest that countries unwilling to resettle refugees provide more generous financial contributions for countries on the front line.

More thought is needed about more robust and creative ways of increased engagement of the private sector, with consideration given to family and community sponsorship opportunities. There are clear disadvantages to having some refugees funded privately while others are funded by a government, but perhaps it is time to take another look at alternative ways of funding resettlement. Could more be done, for example, to strengthen diaspora networks and bring them into the international system? Perhaps they can be considered as potential developmental actors for the reconstruction of their home country when the day comes. Finally, could resettlement to third countries be used for those displaced inside Syria? As noted throughout this report, solutions for IDPs are much more difficult than for refugees. And while countries such as the United States have used in-country processing before, there have been major problems with at least some of these programs (such as in the cases of Haiti and Central America). But in other cases, such as the Orderly Departure Program for Vietnamese in the 1980s, resettlement has saved lives.

The New Global Approach for Syria should provide a new relationship between humanitarian and development actors. Refugees need more opportunities to access education and livelihoods. This means appreciating their economic contributions, and it will require host governments to make difficult decisions to allow them to access employment opportunities. However, it also will be critical that the international community shift gears from an emphasis on short-term humanitarian assistance to long-term development goals. Such a shift has never been done in the midst of ongoing conflict, but there are signs that this may be possible as evidenced by the UN's Regional Refugee and Resilience Plan strategy, the World Bank's new plan for the Middle East and North Africa, and many other initiatives.

It also is important that traditional developmental agencies, led by the World Bank, revise their procedures and make middle-income countries such as Jordan, Lebanon, and Turkey eligible for grants and other support programs. Increasing coordination between these agencies and humanitarian relief agencies will also be critical. These ideas—especially to increase refugees' and their host communities' resilience, and to encourage cooperation with a wider range of stake holders—have indeed been central to the World Bank's new Middle East and North Africa strategy.[41] This in turn could constitute a step in the direction of a Middle East Recovery Plan, a sort of Marshall Plan discussed earlier in this chapter, toward the reconstruction of the region. As one World Bank official explained, it is important to build resilience to communities affected by mass population movements "by supporting the displaced as well as host communities and preparing recovery and reconstruction wherever and whenever peace emerges. This harks back to our immediate post–World War II mission, when we were first established as the IBRD—the International Bank for Reconstruction and Development."[42] Furthermore, going beyond just relief assistance and moving into the developmental aspect of the challenges ahead would also fall in line with the World Bank's recently adopted Sustainable Development Goals.

Indeed, there are a few encouraging signs that development actors, such as the World Bank, are taking steps to play a role in both protracted displacement situations and in supporting solutions for displacement.[43] However, this needs to be robustly supported by political leaders and by the donor community. International agencies beyond UNHCR, the World Food Program, the Office for Coordination of Humanitarian Affairs, and UNICEF will need to become more active, especially the World Bank Group and agencies such as Islamic Development Bank, the European Bank of Reconstruction and Development, and the China-led Asian Infrastructure and Investment Bank. The New Global Approach for Syria should make the engagement of both humanitarian and development actors central.

The New Global Approach for Syria should also offer a forum for creative thinking on solutions for internally displaced people. As this study has shown, internal displacement is directly related to refugee movements; when people cannot find protection within the borders of their own country, they move elsewhere. Protection, assistance, and solutions for IDPs are much more difficult and more controversial than for refugees, and the way forward is much less clear. First and foremost, greater diplomatic efforts should go into strengthening the implementation of earlier UN Security Council resolutions, especially on provision of assistance in rebel-controlled areas. Second, perhaps there are opportunities for engaging the Syrian government around protection of people in besieged areas or in negotiating access. These options should be tried. The "Whole of Syria" approach adopted by the UN in late 2014 offers some important precedents for this. Third, as discussed in chapter 3, challenges and difficulties are associated with "no-fly" and "safe" zones. But these options require further discussion and the elaboration of alternative models for how they can be implemented.

The engagement of different kinds of actors—from experts in peacekeeping to diaspora groups to Gulf charities— may enable more realistic assessments of their possibilities to protect civilians. The New Global Approach for Syria could set up multi-stakeholder working groups that could look at the feasibility of safe zones, no-fly areas, humanitarian corridors, and humanitarian cease-fires. It might be that, as certain parts of Syria achieve relative calm, the idea of extending humanitarian corridors from less secure areas could be considered. In the present political context, there are no good options for responding to IDPs inside Syria or, indeed, to those who are trapped and unable to move. But the New Global Approach for Syria could offer a new space for developing such options and a better forum for coordinating cross-border operations.

The New Global Approach for Syria can include an essential component of preparing the recovery by laying the groundwork for longer-term reconstruction and recovery efforts. Much of this will depend on the political negotiations and the "shape" of a postwar Syria, with the distinct possibility that the contours of the present nation-state of Syria may not remain. But efforts are already under way to think about the transition.[44] These efforts, and many others, could be brought together under the New Global Approach for Syria. Doing so might ensure that humanitarian and development efforts are tailored in such a way to support eventual recovery.

Bringing an end to the conflict in Syria and developing a long-term recovery strategy are clearly the most desired solutions for displacement. Although this ideal appears a distant possibility, it is likely that the eventual shape of postwar

Syria will be determined largely by the patterns of displacement that already have occurred. In this vein, proposals to create safe zones, local cease-fires, and permanent restructuring of the country usually build on the demographic reshaping that has resulted from displacement. A federal or confederal structure may well be the eventual political solution. Some analysts are making the point that it is unlikely Syria will even exist as a nation-state in five years.[45]

Getting to a New Global Approach for Syria

What would a new "Grand Bargain for Syrian Refugees" look like? It would bring together the governments of refugee-hosting countries, the UN and other intergovernmental agencies, regional bodies, international nongovernmental organizations and local civil society actors, and donor governments to consider and adopt a new system of burden sharing. This system potentially would include commitments to keep the borders open to Syrian refugees and to more fairly share the costs of assisting and protecting refugees, along with an agreement to allow Syrian refugees to access education and livelihoods, including through legal employment opportunities.

The process could be jointly organized by the UN secretary general and the president of the World Bank and could culminate in a global meeting in March 2017. That meeting would be intended to ratify the New Global Approach for Syria, which had been worked out through a consultative process with stakeholders over a six-to-twelve-month period. This is a short period of time for international actors to act. But now is not a time for business as usual. The needs are urgent, and with the strong political support of the world's leaders, such a bargain could indeed be pulled off.

We suggest that the UN secretary general and the president of the World Bank announce the initiative at the General Assembly in September 2016 and ask for commitments from stakeholders to actively engage in it. At the same time, the two conveners should announce a list of "expectations," to which relevant stakeholders should respond within a month. For example, one expectation could be that the Organization of Islamic Cooperation would take the lead in organizing a meeting of host-country governments to consider common approaches to the legal status of refugees in their countries and to come up with ways to prevent statelessness among Syrian refugees. Another "expectation" could be for the EU to come up with an implementable "relocation"' policy for Syrian refugees arriving in EU countries. Still another could be to ask the UN Development Program and the Food and Agriculture Organization to compile a list of feasible livelihood projects that could be carried out now in Syria, or to ask UNHCR to put together a concrete proposal to support resettlement of Syrian refugees in countries that have not traditionally resettled refugees.

At the same time as the conveners are launching the New Global Approach for Syria and announcing specific expectations, they should take two additional actions. First, they should commission two definitive studies. One study would cover the positive and negative economic impacts of refugees in host countries; perhaps it could be carried out by a consortium of academic institutions in the region coordinated by the World Bank. The study would also discuss the possibilities in which the creation of livelihood opportunities would connect with an eventual rebuilding program for Syria. A second study should examine the security implications of Syrian refugees; perhaps it could be carried out in association with relevant police associations in the Middle

East, Europe, and elsewhere under the coordination of a respected research institution, perhaps the Stockholm International Peace Research Institute. Other studies may also be needed.

In addition to commissioning studies, the conveners should issue a call to NGOs and civil society organizations, including Muslim charities, to make their contribution to this New Global Approach for Syria. For example, they could solicit the input of refugees and diaspora groups in coming up with less risky paths for Syrians traveling outside the region or in researching coping methods of refugees and identifying measures that could mitigate negative coping behavior, such as early marriage and transactional sex. The possibility of organizing inclusive civil society meetings in the regions, perhaps under the auspices of local universities or NGO platforms, should be considered. There are particular advantages to asking respected groups that are perceived as neutral to play such facilitating roles. The conveners could also set up a website where these contributions could be posted and where collaboration could be sought. Groups of all types—for example, the Intergovernmental Consultations on Migration, Asylum and Refugees; the Red Cross movement; and universities and defense departments—should be encouraged to participate in the process of coming up with a new Grand Bargain for Syrian Refugees.

THE SYRIAN DISPLACEMENT CRISIS AND THE INTERNATIONAL HUMANITARIAN SYSTEM

The international humanitarian system is under serious strain and, as a whole, is overstretched. António Guterres, who just stepped down as UN High Commissioner for Refugees, noted: "If you look at those displaced by conflict per day, in 2010 it was 11,000; last year there were 42,000. This means a dramatic increase in need, from shelter to water and sanitation, food, medical assistance, education." He went on to remark: "The global humanitarian community is not broken—as a whole they are more effective than ever before. But we are financially broke."[46] However, we think that solutions to the problem must involve more than just a simple infusion of funds and that there is a need for more fundamental change to fix the system. With the world's attention now focused on refugees and the Syrian humanitarian crisis generally, this is a perhaps once-in-an-era opportunity to discuss—and implement—bold change to the humanitarian system.

Some of the reflections and consultations in the lead-up to the World Humanitarian Summit offer good proposals for change; for example, the crucial need for more engagement of local civil society actors since local and national humanitarian actors received only 0.2 percent of the overall direct global humanitarian response in 2013.[47] However, these proposals do not go far enough. Bigger issues that need to be addressed include reforming the current Western-led humanitarian system to make sure scarce funds better serve the needy and looking for ways to better integrate the emerging humanitarian actors and donors into a reformed system.[48] Mobilizing collective action on Syria and harnessing the creative energy could well serve as an impetus for more radical change in the international humanitarian system.

The scale of Syrian displacement, the difficulties of accessing people in need inside Syria, and the likelihood that Syrians will be displaced for years are now driving efforts to find political solutions to the conflict. There are risks that this pressure will lead to political agreements that do not offer sufficient protection to those who have been displaced. There also are risks that, given the situation in the neighboring countries and in Europe, refugees will be encouraged or even forced to return home before it is safe for them to do so. Furthermore, as Syrian displacement becomes protracted there is an additional risk that the world's attention will diminish and the crisis will be relegated to situation reports by humanitarian agencies that are read mainly by other humanitarian agencies.

But there is also an opportunity to use this horrific human tragedy to introduce needed fundamental changes to our systems of global governance and humanitarian response. It is an opportunity to bring order out of chaos and, it is hoped, ensure that the victims of the world's next civil conflict will be treated better than the people of Syria have been.

Notes

CHAPTER 1

1. Internal Displacement Monitoring Centre and Norwegian Refugee Council, *Global Overview 2015: People Internally Displaced by Conflict and Violence*, May 6, 2015 (www.internal-displacement.org/assets/library/Media/201505-Global-Overview-2015/201505-Global-Overview-Highlights-document-en.pdf).

2. United Nations High Commissioner for Refugees (UNHCR), "Worldwide Displacement Hits All-Time High as War and Persecution Increase," June 20, 2015 (www.unhcr.org/558193896.html).

3. Erik Melander, "Organized Violence in the World 2015: An Assessment by the Uppsala Conflict Data Program," Uppsala Conflict Data Program, 2015 (www.pcr.uu.se/digitalAssets/61/61335_1ucdp-paper-9.pdf). Also see *Global Peace Index 2015* (http://reliefweb.int/report/world/global-peace-index-2015).

4. Peter Harling and Alex Simon, "The West in the Arab World: Beyond Ennui and Ecstasy," *The Arabist* (blog), December 15, 2015 (http://arabist.net/blog/2015/12/16/the-west-in-the-arab-world-between-ennui-and-ecstasy).

5. Simon Adams, "Failure to Protect: Syria and the UN Security Council," Occasional Paper Series 5, Global Centre for the Responsibility to Protect, March 2015 (www.globalr2p.org/media/files/syriapaper_final.pdf).

6. Dawn Chatty and Nisrine Mansour, "Unlocking Protracted Displacement: An Iraqi Case Study," *Refugee Studies Quarterly* 30, no. 4, November 3, 2011 (http://rsq.oxfordjournals.org/content/30/4/50.abstract).

7. Niels Harild, Asger Christensen, and Roger Zetter, "Sustainable Refugee Return: Triggers, Constraints, and Lessons on Addressing the Development Challenges of Forced Displacement," Global Program on Forced Displacement Issue Series of the World Bank Group, August 2015, p. xi (http://documents.worldbank.org/curated/en/2015/09/25074418/sustainable-refugee-return-triggers-constraints-lessons-addressing-development-challenges-forced-displacement).

8. For earlier reports, see Elizabeth Ferris, Kemal Kirişci, and Salman Shaikh, "Syrian Crisis: Massive Displacement, Dire Needs and Shortage of Solutions," Brookings, September 18, 2013 (www.brookings.edu/research/reports/2013/09/18-syria-humanitarian-political-crisis-ferris-shaikh-kirisci); Osman Bahadır Dinçer, Vittoria Federici, Elizabeth Ferris, Sema Karaca, Kemal Kirişci, and Elif Özmenek Çarmıklı, "Turkey and Syrian Refugees: The Limits of Hospitality," Brookings, November 2013 (www.brookings.edu/research/reports/2013/11/14-syria-turkey-refugees-ferris-kirisci-federici); Kemal Kirişci, "Syrian Refugees and Turkey's Challenges: Going Beyond Hospitality," Brookings-USAK Reports, May 2014 (www.brookings.edu/research/reports/2014/05/12-syrian-refugees-turkeys-challenges-kirisci); Kemal Kirişci and Elizabeth Ferris, "Not Likely to Go Home: Syrian Refugees and the Challenges to Turkey and the International Community," Turkey Project Policy Paper No. 7, Brookings, September 2015 (www.brookings.edu/research/papers/2015/09/syrian-refugee-international-challenges-ferris-kirisci).

9. UNCHR, "The 1951 Refugee Convention" (www.unhcr.org/pages/49da0e466.html).

10. United Nations, Office for the Coordination of Humani-

tarian Affairs, *Guiding Principles on Internal Displacement,* 1998 (www.brookings.edu/~/media/Projects/idp/GPEnglish.pdf).

11. "Palestinian Displacement: A Case Apart?," Special Issue of *Forced Migration Review* 26, August 2006 (www.fmreview.org/en/FMRpdfs/FMR26/FMR26full.pdf). Also see Susan M. Akram, "Reinterpreting Palestinian Refugee Rights under International Law and a Framework for Durable Solutions," *BADIL Briefs* No. 1 (February 2000).

12. For further information on numbers and location of Palestinian refugees today, see United Nations Relief and Work Agency for Palestine Refugees in the Near East, updated on November 9, 2015 (www.unrwa.org/).

13. See, for example, Ahmed Moor, "Lebanon's Law on Palestinian Workers Does Not Go Far Enough," *The Guardian*, August 27, 2010 (www.theguardian.com/commentisfree/2010/aug/27/lebanon-law-palestinian-workers-refugees).

14. Elizabeth Ferris interviews, Beirut, May 2015.

15. The others are voluntary repatriation (also unlikely) and resettlement to a third country, now being discussed more extensively but still unlikely to benefit most Syrian refugees.

16. UNHCR, "UNHCR reports sharp increase in number of Iraqis fleeing to Jordan and Turkey," September 23, 2014 (www.refworld.org/docid/5421775f4.html). For more on Iraqi Christian refugees, see Nigel O'Connor, "Iraq's Christian refugees linger in Jordan," Al Jazeera, December 6, 2014 (www.aljazeera.com/news/middleeast/2014/12/iraq-christian-refugees-linger-jordan-20141247496420774.html).

17. Chatty and Mansour, "Unlocking Protracted Displacement: An Iraqi Case Study," p. 7.

18. "Amid Syrian Crisis, Iraqi Refugees in Jordan Forgotten," *IRIN Reports*, June 6, 2013 (www.irinnews.org/report/98180/amid-syrian-crisis-iraqi-refugees-in-jordan-forgotten).

19. UNHCR, "2015 UNHCR country operations profile—Iraq" (www.unhcr.org/pages/49e486426.html).

20. All figures are based on entries for 2006–13 in the UNHCR Population Statistics Reference Database.

21. United States Citizenship and Immigration Services, "Iraqi Refugee Processing Fact Sheet," last modified June 6, 2013 (www.uscis.gov/humanitarian/refugees-asylum/refugees/iraqi-refugee-processing-fact-sheet).

22. Chatty and Mansour, "Unlocking Protracted Displacement: An Iraqi Case Study," p. 4.

23. Ibid., p. 7.

24. International Crisis Group, *Protest in North Africa and the Middle East (VI): The Syrian People's Slow-Motion Revolution*, p. 11; "Syria Crisis Explained," *Huffington Post,* March 15, 2012 (www.huffingtonpost.com/2012/03/14/syria-crisis-explained_n_1263647.html). Michael S. Doran and Salman Shaikh, "The Ghosts of Hama," in Kenneth M. Pollack, Daniel L. Byman, and others, *The Arab Awakening: America and the Transformation of the Middle East* (Brookings, 2011). Thomas Friedman and others make a convincing case that climate change—and particularly the country's devastating drought between 2006 and 2011 that wiped out the livelihoods of 800,000 Syrian farmers and herders—played a role in the conflict. When people were forced off their land into the cities—and the government did nothing to help their plight—people became politicized. See Thomas Friedman, "Without Water, Revolution," *New York Times*, May 18, 2013 (www.nytimes.com/2013/05/19/opinion/sunday/friedman-without-water-revolution.html?pagewanted=all&_r=1&). Also, Thomas Friedman, "The Other Arab Spring," *New York Times*, April 7, 2012 (www.nytimes.com/2012/04/08/opinion/sunday/friedman-the-other-arab-spring.html); Caitlin E. Werrell and Francesco Femia, eds., *The Arab Spring and Climate Change: A Climate and Security Correlations Series* (Washington, D.C.: Center for American Progress, Stimson Center and the Center for Climate Security, February 2013) (www.americanprogress.org/wp-content/uploads/2013/02/ClimateChangeArabSpring.pdf).

25. Aslı Ilgıt and Rochelle Davis, "The Many Roles of Turkey in the Syrian Crisis," *Middle East Research and Information Project*, January 28, 2013 (www.merip.org/mero/mero012813). Note that small numbers of Syrian refugees were recorded as crossing into Turkey in April 2011.

26. International Crisis Group, "Syria Metastasizing Conflicts," *ICG Middle East Report* 143, June 27, 2013 (www.crisisgroup.org/~/media/Files/Middle%20East%20North%20Africa/Iraq%20Syria%20Lebanon/Syria/143-syrias-metastasising-conflicts.pdf).

27. UN Human Rights Council, "Report of the Independent International Commission of Inquiry on the Syrian Arab Republic," A/HRC/30/48, August 13, 2015 (www.ohchr.org/EN/HR Bodies/HRC/IICISyria/Pages/Documentation.aspx).

28. International Crisis Group, "Syria's Metastasizing Conflicts," p. ii. For the complicated and constantly shifting political scene in Syria, see Liz Sly, "Is It Too Late to Solve the Mess in the Middle East?," *Washington Post,* November 17, 2015 (www.washingtonpost.com/world/the-long-war-against-islamist-extremism-has-become-more-complicated-than-ever/2015/11/17/0b255c26-8c8e-11e5-934c-a369c80822c2_story.html).

29. "Foreign Fighters: An Update," *The Soufan Group IntelBriefs*, December 8, 2015 (http://soufangroup.com/tsg-intelbrief-foreign-fighters-an-update/); Christopher M. Blanchard, Carla Humud, and Mary Beth D. Nikitin, "Armed Conflict in Syria: Overview and U.S. Response," *Congressional Research Service Reports,* October 9, 2015 (www.fas.org/sgp/crs/mideast/RL33487.pdf).

30. Emile Hokayem, *Syria's Uprising and the Fracturing of the Levant* (Abingdon, Oxon: Routledge for the International Institute for Strategic Studies, 2013), p. 17.

31. Carsten Wieland, *Syria—A Decade of Lost Chances: Repression and Revolution from Damascus Spring to Arab Spring* (Seattle: Cune Press, 2012), p. 86.

32. Elizabeth Ferris and Kemal Kirişci, interviews, June 2015. Also see Guilllaume Charron, "Syria: Forsaken IDPs adrift inside a Fragmenting State," Internal Displacement Monitoring Centre, October 21, 2014 (www.internal-displacement.org/middle-east-and-north-africa/syria/2014/syria-forsaken-idps-adrift-inside-a-fragmenting-state).

33. UN Human Rights Council, "Report of the Independent International Commission of Inquiry on the Syrian Arab Republic," A/HRC/30/48, August 13, 2015, p. 15 (www.ohchr.org/

EN/HRBodies/HRC/IICISyria/Pages/IndependentInternational Commission.aspx).

34. Ibid., p. 39.

35. David Lesch, *Syria: The Fall of the House of Assad* (Yale University Press, 2012), pp. 106–07.

36. "Houla: How a Massacre Unfolded," BBC News, June 8, 2012 (www.bbc.com/news/world-middle-east-18233934).

37. Hugh Naylor, "Some Alawites Are Beginning to Question Their Support for Syria's Assad," *Washington Post*, November 12, 2014 (www.washingtonpost.com/world/middle_east/some-alawites-are-beginning-to-question-their-support-for-syrias-assad/2014/11/11/ee302b0c-aac0-4f17-a220-cddcd49b52db_story.html).

38. Aron Lund, "Abu Mohammed Al-Golani's Al Jazeera Interview," May 29, 2015 (www.joshualandis.com/blog/abu-moham med-al-golanis-aljazeera-interview-by-aron-lund/).

39. Bob Bowker, "Syria: World dithers as new refugee crisis looms," *Lowy Interpreter*, July 15, 2015 (www.lowyinterpreter.org/post/2015/07/15/Syria-World-dithers-as-new-refugee-crisis-looms.aspx).

40. "Syria's Beleaguered Christians," BBC News, February 25, 2015 (www.bbc.com/news/world-middle-east-22270455).

41. Economist Intelligence Unit, "Syria Report," *The Economist,* July 2015.

42. Hokayem, *Syria's Uprising and the Fracturing of the Levant*, p. 44.

43. Lina Sinjab, "Syria's Minorities Drawn into Conflict," BBC News, August 22, 2012 (www.bbc.com/news/world-middle-east-19319448).

44. Aryn Baker, "Eyewitness from Homs: An Alawite Refugee Warns of Sectarian War in Syria," *Time*, March 1, 2012 (http://world.time.com/2012/03/01/eyewitness-from-homs-an-alawite-refugee-warns-of-sectarian-war-in-syria/).

45. "Syria's Beleaguered Christians," BBC News.

46. "Battle for Syrian Christian Town of Maaloula Continues," BBC News, September 11, 2013 (www.bbc.com/news/world-middle-east-24051440).

47. "Islamic State: Fears Grow for Abducted Syrian Christians," BBC News, February 25, 2015 (www.bbc.com/news/world-middle-east-31622883).

48. Human Rights Watch, "Syria: Rebels' Car Bombs, Rockets Kill Civilians," March 22, 2015 (www.hrw.org/report/2015/03/22/he-didnt-have-die/indiscriminate-attacks-opposition-groups-syria?_ga=1.258506829.616246348.1430244874).

49. Ibid.

50. "Islamic State: Fears Grow for Abducted Syrian Christians," BBC News.

51. "Guide: Syria's Diverse Minorities," BBC News, December 9, 2011 (www.bbc.com/news/world-middle-east-16108755).

52. Tom Perry and Suleiman al-Khalidi, "Calls for Aid to Syria's Druze after al-Qaeda Kills 20," Reuters, June 11, 2015 (www.reuters.com/article/2015/06/11/us-mideast-crisis-druze-idUSKBN0OR0NV20150611).

53. Nikolaos van Dam, *The Struggle for Power in Syria: Politics and Society under Asad and the Ba'ath Party* (London: IB Tauris, 1997), p. 6.

54. Ibid., p. 15.

55. Yaniv Kubovich, Jack Khoury, Gili Cohen, and Jonathan Lis, "Israel Preparing for Possible Influx of Syrian Refugees," *Haaretz*, June 17, 2015 (www.haaretz.com/israel-news/.premium-1.661603).

56. Faisal Irshaid, "Syria's Druze under Threat as Conflict Spreads," BBC News, June 19, 2015 (www.bbc.com/news/world-middle-east-33166043); and Ariel Ben Solomon, "Syrian Druze form security force as trust wanes in Assad," *Jerusalem Post*, January 13, 2016 (www.jpost.com/Middle-East/Syrian-Druse-form-security-force-as-trust-wanes-in-Assad-to-protect-them-from-ISIS-441406).

57. "Don't Bruise the Druze," *The Economist*, June 20, 2015 (www.economist.com/news/middle-east-and-africa/21654660-israel-has-warned-syrian-rebels-steer-clear-one-particular-minority-dont).

58. Nicholas Blanford, "For Syria's Druze, Survival Hinges on Choosing the Right Ally," Al Jazeera America, July 2, 2015 (http://

america.aljazeera.com/articles/2015/7/2/druze-struggle-for-survival-in-syria.html).

59. Hugh Naylor, "In New Signs of Assad's Troubles, Syria's Druze Turn Away from President," *Washington Post*, July 20, 2015 (www.washingtonpost.com/world/middle_east/in-new-sign-of-assads-troubles-syrias-druze-turn-away-from-president/2015/07/17/eaf06874-18f7-11e5-bed8-1093ee58dad0_story.html).

60. Ibid.

61. International Crisis Group, "Uncharted Waters: Thinking through Syria's Dynamics," *ICG Middle East Policy Briefing* 31, November 24, 2011, p. 3 (www.crisisgroup.org/~/media/Files/Middle%20East%20North%20Africa/Iraq%20Syria%20Lebanon/Syria/B031%20Uncharted%20Waters%20-%20Thinking%20Through%20Syrias%20Dynamics.pdf).

62. International Organization for Migration Iraq Mission, "Iraq's Crisis Report," *Situation Update* 26, October 15, 2015 (http://iomiraq.net/article/0/iraq-crisis-situation-report-16-september-15-october).

63. Internal Displacement Monitoring Centre, "Iraq IDP Figures Analysis," June 15, 2015 (www.internal-displacement.org/middle-east-and-north-africa/iraq/figures-analysis).

64. "Survival on Sinjar Mountain," *IRIN News*, October 22, 2015 (http://newirin.irinnews.org/survival-on-sinjar-mountain/). See also "Reports Reveal the Plight of Yazidi Refugees in Turkey," *Hurriyet Daily News*, July 9, 2015 (www.hurriyetdailynews.com/report-reveals-plight-of-yazidi-refugees-in-turkey.aspx?PageID=238&NID=85163&NewsCatID=341).

65. See, for example, Rukmini Callimachi, "ISIS Enshrines a Theology of Rape," *New York Times*, August 13, 2015 (www.nytimes.com/2015/08/14/world/middleeast/isis-enshrines-a-theology-of-rape.html?_r=0).

66. "Iraq Crisis—Ramadi Displacement," OCHA Flash Update, June 1–3, 2015 (http://reliefweb.int/sites/reliefweb.int/files/resources/ocha_flash_update_no._9-_iraq_crisis_-_ramadi_displacement-_1-3_june_2015.pdf).

67. "Iraq on the Brink of Humanitarian Disaster Due to Surging Conflict and Massive Funding Shortfalls Warns UN," UNICEF

Press Center (www.unicef.org/media/media_82175.html). Also see Omar Al-Jawoshy, "Iraq: Funding Shortfall Deprives Uprooted Iraqis of Health Services," *New York Times*, August 13, 2015 (www.nytimes.com/2015/08/05/world/middleeast/iraq-funding-shortfall-deprives-uprooted-iraqis-of-health-services.html).

68. "Syrian Regime Bombing Kills over 5000 in 10 Months," *Al-Araby al-Jadeed* [New Arab], August 20, 2015 (www.alaraby.co.uk/english/news/2015/8/20/syrian-regime-bombing-kills-over-5000-in-ten-months).

69. Kareem Fahim and Maher Samaan, "Violence in Syria Spurs a Huge Surge in Civilian Flight," *New York Times*, October 26, 2015 (www.nytimes.com/2015/10/27/world/middleeast/syria-russian-air-strike-refugees.html?_r=0); and Liz Sly, "Russian Airstrikes Force a Halt to Aid in Syria, Triggering a New Crisis," *Washington Post,* December 14, 2015 (www.washingtonpost.com/world/middle_east/russian-airstrikes-force-a-halt-to-aid-in-syria-triggering-a-new-crisis/2015/12/14/cebc4b66-9f87-11e5-9ad2-568d814bbf3b_story.html).

70. UN Human Rights Council, "Report of the Independent International Commission of Inquiry on the Syrian Arab Republic," A/HRC/23/58, June 4, 2013, para. 91 (www.ohchr.org/Documents/HRBodies/HRCouncil/CoISyria/A-HRC-23-58_en.pdf).

71. Ibid., paras. 149–51.

72. International Crisis Group, "Uncharted Waters: Thinking through Syria's Dynamics," p. 6.

73. Jihad Yazigi, "Syria's War Economy," *Policy Briefs*, European Council on Foreign Relations, April 2014, p. 1 (www.ecfr.eu/page/-/ECFR97_SYRIA_BRIEF_AW.pdf p. 1); and United Nations Economic and Social Commission for Western Asia, "Syrian Experts Urge Geneva II Parties to Seize Historic Opportunity," January 21, 2104 (www.escwa.un.org/information/pressescwa print.asp?id_code=610).

74. UN Human Rights Council, "Report of the Independent International Commission of Inquiry on the Syrian Arab Republic," August 13, 2015, pp. 7–8.

75. Rochelle Davis, Abbie Taylor, and Emma Murphy, "Gender, Conscription and Protection, and the War in Syria," *Forced Migra-*

tion Review 47, September 2014 (www.fmreview.org/syria/davis-taylor-murphy).

76. UN Human Rights Council, "Report of the Independent International Commission of Inquiry on the Syrian Arab Republic," A/HRC/30/48, August 13, 2015, p. 8 (www.ohchr.org/EN/HRBodies/HRC/IICISyria/Pages/IndependentInternationalCommission.aspx).

77. Ibid.

78. Ibid.

79. UNHCR, Refugees/Migrants Emergency Response–Mediterranean (http://data.unhcr.org/mediterranean/regional.php).

80. "2015 Global Appeal: $16.7 Billion to Help 57 Million People in 22 Countries," OCHA, December 8, 2014 (www.unocha.org/top-stories/all-stories/2015-global-appeal-164-billion-help-57-million-people-22-countries).

CHAPTER 2

1. "Syria Regional Refugee Response," United Nations High Commissioner for Refugees (http://data.unhcr.org/syrianrefugees/regional.php). This figure is for March 31, 2012.

2. Ibid.

3. "Syria Regional Response Plan: Lebanon," United Nations High Commissioner for Refugees, updated on December 31, 2015 (http://data.unhcr.org/syrianrefugees/country.php?id=122); "Syria Regional Response Plan: Jordan," ibid., updated on December 17, 2015 (http://data.unhcr.org/syrianrefugees/country.php?id=107).

4. "Syria Regional Response Plan: Turkey," United Nations High Commissioner for Refugees, updated on December 31, 2015 (http://data.unhcr.org/syrianrefugees/country.php?id=224).

5. Lorne Cook, "Turkey Warns EU that 3 Million More Refugees Could Leave Syria," *Global News*, October 6, 2015 (http://globalnews.ca/news/2260726/turkey-warns-eu-that-3-million-more-refugees-could-leave-syria/); and Kareem Fahim and Maher Samaan, "Violence in Syria Spurs a Huge Surge in Civilian Fight,"

New York Times, October 26, 2015 (www.nytimes.com/2015/10/27/
world/middleeast/syria-russian-air-strike-refugees.html). The UN
Office for the Coordination of Humanitarian Affairs noted that
120,000 were displaced as a result of recent fighting and another
700,000 Syrians could be displaced, in "Syrian Arab Republic: Development in Northern Governorates—Situation Report No. 1," October 24, 2015 (www.humanitarianresponse.info/en/system/files/
documents/files/syria_northern_governorates_situation_report_
final.pdf).

6. Calculated from UNHCR data (http://data.unhcr.org/
syrianrefugees/country.php?id=224).

7. Ahmet İçduygu, *Syrian Refugees in Turkey: The Long Road
Ahead* (Washington, D.C.: Migration Policy Institute, 2015).

8. Elizabeth Ferris and Kemal Kirişci, interviews with officials
and NGO representatives in Turkey, June 15–19, 2015.

9. "Syria's Turkmen ask for Turkey's help under heavy bombardment by Russia," *Today's Zaman,* November 22, 2015 (www.
todayszaman.com/diplomacy_syrian-turkmens-ask-for-turkeys-
help-under-heavy-bombardment-by-assad-russia_404962.html).

10. "Russian Airstrikes Force a Halt in Syria, Triggering a New
Crisis," *Washington Post,* December 14, 2015 (www.washington-
post.com/world/middle_east/russian-airstrikes-force-a-halt-to-
aid-in-syria-triggering-a-new-crisis/2015/12/14/cebc4b66-9f
87-11e5-9ad2-568d814bbf3b_story.html).

11. M. Murat Erdoğan and Can Ünver, "Perspectives, Expectations and Suggestions of the Turkish Business Sector on Syrians
in Turkey," Turkish Confederation of Employer Associations, December 2015, p. 80 (https://mmuraterdogan.files.wordpress.com/
2016/01/syrians-eng-mme.pdf).

12. Kemal Kirişci and Elizabeth Ferris, "Not Likely to Go Home:
Syrian Refugees and the Challenges to Turkey—and the International Community," Turkey Project Policy Paper No. 7, Brookings,
September 2015 (www.brookings.edu/research/papers/2015/09/
syrian-refugee-international-challenges-ferris-kirisci).

13. Kemal Kirişci, "Syrian Refugees and Turkey's Challenges:
Going Beyond Hospitality," Brookings, May 2014, p. 18 (www.

brookings.edu/research/reports/2014/05/12-syrian-refugees-turkeys-challenges-kirisci).

14. Aaron Stein, "For Turkey, It's All about Regime Change in Syria," Al Jazeera, October 8, 2014 (www.aljazeera.com/indepth/opinion/2014/10/turkey-it-all-about-regime-chan-20141078565 6887159.html).

15. Brian Whitaker, "Syria Crisis: Turkey Calls for 'Safe Haven,'" *The Guardian*, August 31, 2012 (www.theguardian.com/world/middle-east-live/2012/aug/31/syria-crisis-bashar-al-assad).

16. Kemal Kirişci, interviews conducted with international nongovernmental organizations in Amman, October 4–6, 2015.

17. Amnesty International, *Fears and Fences: Europe's Approach to Keeping Refugees at Bay* (London: Amnesty International, November 2015). A Human Rights Watch report raised growing concerns about Syrian refugees being denied entry into Turkey as the government tightened border security after ISIS attacks; see Human Rights Watch, "Turkey: Syrians Pushed Back at the Border," November 23, 2015 (www.hrw.org/news/2015/11/23/turkey-syrians-pushed-back-border).

18. Melih Aslan, "Migrants Fleeing Syria Encounter a Life of Detention in Turkey," *Washington Post*, December 27, 2015 (www.washingtonpost.com/world/migrants-fleeing-syria-encounter-a-life-of-detention-in-turkey/2015/12/27/3f63ce4c-acdb-11e5-9ab0-884d1cc4b33e_story.html); see also Human Rights Watch, "Turkey: Syrians Pushed Back at the Border" and Louisa Loveluck, "Turkey 'Turning away All Syrians Who Try to Cross the Border,'" *Daily Telegraph*, November 23, 2015 (www.telegraph.co.uk/news/worldnews/europe/turkey/12012932/Turkey-turning-away-all-Syrians-who-try-to-cross-border.html).

19. Michael Pizzi, "In Syria's War Refugees, Lebanon Sees Echoes of Palestinian Crisis," Al Jazeera America, February 6, 2015 (http://america.aljazeera.com/articles/2015/1/6/lebanon-syria-refugees.html).

20. Nour Samaha, "'I Wasn't Afraid, but Now I Am': Syrians Fear Lebanon's Visa Rules," Al Jazeera America, January 5, 2015 (http://america.aljazeera.com/articles/2015/1/5/syria-refugees-lebanon.

html); "Syria Regional Response Plan: Lebanon," United Nations High Commissioner for Refugees, updated on September 30, 2015 (http://data.unhcr.org/syrianrefugees/country.php?id=122).

21. Liz Sly, "As Tragedies Shock Europe, a Bigger Refugee Crisis Looms in the Middle East," *Washington Post,* August 29, 2015 (www.washingtonpost.com/world/middle_east/as-tragedies-shock-europe-a-bigger-refugee-crisis-looms-in-the-middle-east/2015/08/29/3858b284-9c15-11e4-86a3-1b56f64925f6_story.html); and Hugh Naylor and Susan Haidamous, "Syrian Refugees Become Less Welcome in Lebanon, as New Entry Rules Take Effect," *Washington Post,* January 5, 2015 (www.washingtonpost.com/world/syrian-refugees-become-less-welcome-in-lebanon-as-new-entry-rules-take-effect/2015/01/05/7e412f59-b357-4af4-95a4-5edf3df7af06_story.html). The desperate nature of the situation is also raised by Oxfam in "Lebanon: Looking Ahead in Times of Crisis," Oxfam Discussion Paper, December 2015, p. 19 (www.oxfam.org/en/research/lebanon-looking-ahead-times-crisis).

22. Carole Alsharabati and Jihad Nammour, *Survey on Perceptions of Syrian Refugees in Lebanon* (Beirut: Institute des Sciences Politiques—USJ, 2015).

23. Semih Idiz, "Attacks on Syrians in Turkey Increasing," *Al-Monitor,* May 20, 2015 (www.al-monitor.com/pulse/originals/2015/05/turkey-attack-on-syrians-in-country-on-the-rise.html); for a detailed survey of such incidents, see Oytun Orhan and Sabiha Şenyücel Gündoğar, "Effects of the Syrian Refugees on Turkey," *Orsam Report* No. 195, January 2015, pp. 21–32.

24. M. Murat Erdoğan, *Syrians in Turkey: Social Acceptance and Integration Research* (Ankara: Hacettepe University, January 2015), p. 68.

25. Mona Christopherson, Catherine Moe Thorleifsson, and Age A. Tiltnes, "Ambivalent Hospitality: Coping Strategies and Local Responses to Syrian Refugees in Lebanon," FAFO Foundation Studies, May 2013 (www.fafo.no/ais/middeast/lebanon/91369-syrian-refugees.html).

26. Alsharabati and Nammour, *Survey on Perception of Syrian Refugees in Lebanon,* pp. 8 and 21.

27. Kemal Kirişci, interview conducted at the Center for Strategic Studies at the University of Jordan, Amman, October 5, 2015; Elizabeth Ferris, interviews with UN officials in Beirut, June 9, 2015.

28. This sentiment was expressed to the authors of this book by practically every NGO and municipality person interviewed during their June 10–19, 2015, trip to Turkey as well as their trips to Lebanon in June 2015 and Jordan in October 2015. This problem has been highlighted by numerous reports, for example, Orhan and Şenyücel Gündoğar, "Effects of the Syrian Refugees on Turkey," and Kılıç Buğra Kanat and Kadir Üstün, "Turkey's Syrian Refugees: Toward Integration," *SETA Report*, May 2015 (http://setadc. org/wp-content/uploads/2015/05/Turkeys-Syrian-Refugees.pdf); and International Republican Institute, "Survey of Jordan Political Opinion: February 25—March 1, 2015," May 26, 2015 (www.iri. org/sites/default/files/wysiwyg/2015-05-26_survey_of_jordanian_ public_opinion_february_25-march_1_2015.pdf).

29. Erdoğan, *Syrians in Turkey*, p. 66.

30. "Lebanon: Syrian Refugees Cost the Economy $4.5 Billion Every Year," *Fanack Chronicle*, June 23, 2015 (https://chronicle. fanack.com/lebanon/economy/lebanon-syrian-refugees-cost-the- economy-4-5-billion-every-year/).

31. Kemal Kirişci, interview conducted at Hashemite Charity Organization, Amman, October 6, 2015.

32. For an early appraisal of the challenges, see International Labor Organization, "Assessment of the Impact of Syrian Refugees in Lebanon and Their Employment Profile," April 2014 (www. ilo.org/beirut/publications/WCMS_240134/lang--en/index.htm); see also Saleem Aljuni and Mary Kawar, "Towards Decent Work in Lebanon: Issues and Challenges in Light of the Syrian Refugee Crisis," International Labor Organization, June 2015 (www.ilo. org/wcmsp5/groups/public/---arabstates/---ro-beirut/docu- ments/publication/wcms_374826.pdf); "Access to Work for Syrian Refugees in Jordan," International Labor Organization, 2015 (www.ilo.org/wcmsp5/groups/public/---arabstates/---ro-beirut/ documents/publication/wcms_357950.pdf); and Svein Erik Stave and Solveig Hillesund, "Impact of Syrian Refugees on the Jorda-

nian Labor Market," FAFO Foundation, 2015 (http://reliefweb.int/
sites/reliefweb.int/files/resources/ImpactofSyrianrefugeesonthe-
Jordanianlabourmarket.pdf).

33. Erdoğan, *Syrians in Turkey,* p. 67.

34. Alsharabati and Nammour, *Survey on Perception of Syrian Refugees in Lebanon,* p. 21.

35. Mageed Yahia, "WFP Jordan: Brief," World Food Program, October 2015 (http://documents.wfp.org/stellent/groups/public/
documents/ep/wfp274960.pdf).

36. Ximena V. Del Carpio and Mathis Wagner, "The Impact of Syrian Refugees on Turkish Labor Market," World Bank Working Paper, August 2015 (https://openknowledge.worldbank.org/bit-
stream/handle/10986/22659/The0impact0of00Turkish0labor
0market.pdf?sequence=1&isAllowed=y); "Turkey's Response to the Syrian Refugee Crisis and the Road Ahead," *World Bank Reports,* December 2015, p. 2 (www-wds.worldbank.org/external/
default/WDSContentServer/WDSP/IB/2015/12/21/090224b08
3ed7485/1_0/Rendered/PDF/Turkey0s0respo0s0and0the0
road0ahead.pdf); Massimiliano Cali, Wissam Harake, Fadi Hassan, and Clemens Struck, "The Impact of the Syrian Conflict on Lebanese Trade," *World Bank Reports,* April 2015 (https://
openknowledge.worldbank.org/bitstream/handle/10986/21914/
The0impact0of00ct0on0Lebanese0trade.pdf?sequence=1&is
Allowed=y); and Elena Ianchovichina and Maros Ivanic, "Economic Effects of the Syrian War and the Spread of the Islamic State on the Levant," World Bank Working Paper, December 2014 (https://openknowledge.worldbank.org/bitstream/handle/10986
/20696/WPS7135.pdf?sequence=1&isAllowed=y).

37. These figures for Gaziantep, Kilis, Mersin, and Şanlıurfa provinces were calculated from the data made available by the Turkish Statistical Institute. The total of these exports for these four provinces for 2011 stood at $177 million and $542 million in 2014. The growing number of firms set up by Syrian business people, especially in Mersin, with connections in Syria is also seen as a factor that has helped increase exports. For this issue, see Orhan and Şenyücel Gündoğar, "Effects of the Syrian Refugees on Turkey"; and David Butter, "Syria's Economy: Picking up the Pieces," Cha-

tham House Research Paper, June 2015, p. 26. (www.chatham house.org/sites/files/chathamhouse/field/field_document/201506 23SyriaEconomyButter.pdf).

38. Figures have been calculated based on the UN's COM-TRADE database. Lebanon's exports to Syria steadily increased from $214 million in 2011 to $241 million in 2014 with a peak of more than $500 million in 2013, while Jordan's exports initially fell from $318 million in 2011 to $170 million in 2013, but climbed up to $247 million in 2014.

39. Calculated from tables on pp. 9–10 in Esra Özpınar, Seda Başıhoş, and Aycan Kulaksız, "Trade Relations with Syria after the Refugee Influx," *Evaluation Note,* Economic Policy Research Foundation of Turkey, November 11, 2015 (www.tepav.org.tr/en/haberler/s/3950).

40. Erdoğan and Ünver, "Perspectives, Expectations and Suggestions of the Turkish Business Sector on Syrians in Turkey," p. 52.

41. Yusuf Mansur, "Let Them Work," *Venture Magazine,* May 10, 2015 (www.venturemagazine.me/2015/05/let-them-work/); see also Massimiliano Carli and Samia Sekkarie, "Much Ado about Nothing?: The Economic Impact of Refugee 'Invasions,'" *Future Developments: Economics to End Poverty* (blog), September 16, 2015 (www.brookings.edu/blogs/future-development/posts/2015/09/16-economic-impact-refugees-cali).

42. Elizabeth Ferris and Kemal Kirişci, interview in Gaziantep, June 17, 2015.

43. Nina Strochlic, "Jordan Squeezes Syrian Refugees, Pushing Them back Towards Hell," *The Daily Beast,* May 1, 2015 (www.thedailybeast.com/articles/2015/05/01/jordan-squeezes-syrian-refugees-pushing-them-back-toward-hell.html).

44. "Child Marriages Double among Syria Refugees in Jordan," Al Arabiya, July 16, 2014 (http://english.alarabiya.net/en/News/middle-east/2014/07/16/Child-marriages-double-among-Syria-refugees-in-Jordan-.html); "Too Young to Wed: The Growing Problem of Child Marriage among Syrian Girls in Jordan," Save the Children, July 17, 2014 (www.savethechildren.org/atf/cf/%7B9def2ebe-10ae-432c-9bd0-df91d2eba74a%7D/TOO_

YOUNG_TO_WED_REPORT_0714.PDF); Dominique Soguel, "In Turkey, Syrian Women and Girls Increasingly Vulnerable to Exploitation," *Christian Science Monitor,* October 26, 2014 (www. csmonitor.com/World/Middle-East/2014/1026/In-Turkey-Syrian-women-and-girls-increasingly-vulnerable-to-exploitation); and Eleanor Goldberg, "Struggling Syrian Refugee Girls in Lebanon often Resort to Marriage: Here is who's helping," *Huffington Post,* October 16, 2015.

45. On the court decision, see Riada Asimovic Akyol, "Turkish Court Stirs Marriage Debate," *Al-Monitor,* June 1, 2015 (www.al-monitor.com/pulse/tr/contents/articles/originals/2015/06/turkey-top-court-stirs-debate-on-religious-marriage.html); and Xanthe Ackerman, "In Turkey: Rolling Back Protections for Women," Middle East Institute, September 18, 2015 (www.mei.edu/content/article/turkey-rolling-back-protections-women).

46. *Right to a Future,* Joint Agency Briefing Paper, November 9, 2015 (www.oxfam.org/sites/www.oxfam.org/files/file_attachme nts/bp-right-to-future-syria-refugees-091115-en.pdf).

47. M. Murat Erdoğan, *Türkiye'deki Suriyeliler: Toplumsal Kabul ve Uyum* [Syrians in Turkey: social acceptance and integration] (Istanbul: Istanbul Bilgi Universitesi Yayınları, 2015), p. 13; Erdoğan noted that the public opinion survey revealed a strong relationship between attitudes toward Syrian refugees and the government's handling of the crisis and political party allegiances. Other surveys also captured this relationship. See, for example, *Türk Kamuoyunun Suriyeli Sığınmacılara Yönelik Bakış Açısı* [Turkish public opinion regarding Syrian refugees], EDAM: Türkiye Dış Politika ve Kamuoyu Araştırma Anketleri [Foreign policy and public opinion surveys], January 2014 (http://edam.org.tr/media/icerikfiles/12/edamanket2014.1.pdf); Orhan and Şenyücel Gündoğar, "Effects of the Syrian Refugees on Turkey," also noted the relationship between views on Syrian refugees in Turkey and political affiliations in Turkey.

48. For Alevi and Kurdish concerns, see Kirişci, "Syrian Refugees and Turkey's Challenges: Going beyond Hospitality," pp. 30–34. See also Soner Cagaptay, "The Impact of Syria's Refugees on Southern Turkey," *Policy Focus* 130, Washington Institute for Near East

Policy, July 2014 (www.washingtoninstitute.org/uploads/Docu
ments/pubs/PolicyFocus130_Cagaptay_Revised3s.pdf).

49. Erdoğan, *Türkiye'deki Suriyeliler*, p. 13.

50. Amberin Zaman, "Can Turkey Pull Back from the Brink
of Civil Conflict?," *Al-Monitor*, September 11, 2015 (www.al-
monitor.com/pulse/originals/2015/09/turkey-pkk-clashes-pull-
back-from-brink-of-civil-conflict.html#); and Ceylan Yeginsu,
"Turkey's Campaign against Kurdish Militants Takes Toll on
Civilians," *New York Times*, December 30, 2015 (www.nytimes.
com/2015/12/31/world/europe/turkey-kurds-pkk.html?_r=0).

51. Kemal Kirişci and Sinan Ekim, "Is Civil War Coming to
Turkey?," *Order from Chaos* (blog), September 23, 2015 (www.
brookings.edu/blogs/order-from-chaos/posts/2015/09/23-is-
turkey-civil-war-coming-kirisci-ekim).

52. Michael Karam, "How Lebanon Is Coping with More than
a Million Refugees," *The Spectator*, November 14, 2015 (http://
new.spectator.co.uk/2015/11/how-lebanon-is-coping-with-more-
than-a-million-syrian-refugees/); and Anne Bernard and Julien
Barnes-Dacey, "Lebanon: Resilience Meets Its Stiffest Test," in *The
Regional Struggle for Syria*, edited by Barnes-Dacey and Daniel
Levy (London: European Council on Foreign Relations, July 2013),
p. 61–67.

53. Marisa Sullivan, "Hezbollah in Syria," Institute for the
Study of War, *Middle East Security Report* No. 19, April 2014
(www.understandingwar.org/sites/default/files/Hezbollah_Sul-
livan_FINAL.pdf).

54. Anatolia News Agency, "Syrian Rebels Attack Hezbollah's
Positions in Lebanon: FSA Commander," *Hürriyet Daily News*,
February 21, 2013 (www.hurriyetdailynews.com/syrian-rebels-
attack-hezbollahs-positions-in-lebanon-fsa-commander.aspx?
pageID=238&nid=41647); and "Hezbollah Repel Syrian Rebel
Attack on Lebanon-Syria Border," *MintPress News*, October 6, 2014
(www.mintpressnews.com/hezbollah-repel-syirn-rebel-attack
-on-lebanon-syria-border/197331/).

55. Natasha Smith, "The Complexities in Lebanon," *Fair Ob-
server*, May 31, 2012 (www.fairobserver.com/region/middle_east_
north_africa/the-complexities-of-lebanon/); and David Schenker, "How

Syria's Civil War Threatens Lebanon's Fragile Peace," *Los Angeles Times,* April 1, 2014 (http://articles.latimes.com/2014/apr/01/opinion/la-oe-schenker-lebanon-forces-20140401); and Haytham Mouzahem, "Tripoli: A Reflection of Syria's Sectarian War," *Al-Monitor,* May 25, 2013 (www.al-monitor.com/pulse/fr/originals/2013/05/lebanon-tripoli-syria-crisis.html#).

56. Anne Barnard, "Beirut, also the Site of Deadly Attacks, Feels Forgotten," *New York Times,* November 15, 2015 (www.nytimes.com/2015/11/16/world/middleeast/beirut-lebanon-attacks-paris.html?_r=0).

57. Bassel Salloukh, "Syria and Lebanon: A Brotherhood Transformed," Middle East Research and Information Project, Summer 2015 (www.merip.org/mer/mer236/syria-lebanon-brotherhood-transformed). The Syrian notion of "Greater Syria" included Lebanon; for more on this, see Malik Mufti, *Sovereign Creations: Pan-Arabism and Political Order in Syria and Iraq* (Cornell University Press, 1996).

58. Salloukh, "Syria and Lebanon: A Brotherhood Transformed."

59. Michael Pizzi, "In Syria's War Refugees, Lebanon Sees Echoes of Palestinian Crisis," Al Jazeera America, January 6, 2015 (http://america.aljazeera.com/articles/2015/1/6/lebanon-syria-refugees.html). For the Lebanese civil war and its impact on Lebanon, see William Harris, "Republic of Lebanon," in *The Government and Politics of the Middle East and North Africa,* edited by Mark Gasiorowski (Boulder, Colo.: Westview Press, 2014).

60. For the Jordanian civil war and its impact on Jordan, see Curtis R. Ryan, "Hashimite Kingdom of Jordan" in *The Government and Politics of the Middle East and North Africa,* edited by Gasiorowski.

61. Kemal Kirişci, "'Coerced Immigrants': Refugees of Turkish Origins since 1945," *International Migration* 34, no. 3 (1996).

62. In 2014 Turkey was, after Russia, Germany, and the United States, the fourth largest recipient of individual asylum applications filed by nationals coming from third countries other than Syria; see "World at War: Forced Displacement in 2014," *UNHCR Global Trends,* June 19, 2015, pp. 28–29 (www.unhcr.org/556725e69.html).

63. See Article 1 of the 1951 Convention on the Status of Refugees (www.unhcr.org/3b66c2aa10.html).

64. İçduygu, *Syrian Refugees in Turkey: The Long Road Ahead.*

65. European Commission, "Turkey Report 2015," EC Commission Staff Working Documents, November 10, 2015, p. 71.

66. Ala Alrababah and Ghazi Jarrar, "Syrian Refugees: Time to Do the Right Thing," Sharnoff's Global Views, August 18, 2013 (www.sharnoffsglobalviews.com/jordan-syrian-refugees-162/).

67. The shortage of water and its implications were frequently raised during interviews with Jordanian officials as well as representatives of international agencies, in particular International Committee of the Red Cross and the Swiss Cooperation Office; Kemal Kirişci, interviews conducted in Amman, Jordan, October 4–6, 2015.

68. King Abdullah, "Remarks by His Majesty King Abdullah II at the Plenary Session at the 70th General Assembly of the United Nations," September 28, 2015 (http://kingabdullah.jo/index.php/en_US/speeches/view/id/565/videoDisplay/0.html).

69. Doris Carrion, "Syrian Refugees in Jordan: Confronting Difficult Truths," Chatham House Research Paper, September 2015 (www.chathamhouse.org/sites/files/chathamhouse/field/field_document/20150921SyrianRefugeesCarrion.pdf).

70. Saleh Al-Kilani, "A Duty and a Burden on Jordan," *Forced Migration Review,* September 2014 (www.fmreview.org/syria/al-kilani).

71. Hashemite Kingdom of Jordan, Ministry of Planning and International Cooperation, Jordan Response Plan for the Syria Crisis, 2016–2018, released 2015. See the plan at http://static1.squarespace.com/static/522c2552e4b0d3c39ccd1e00/t/56b9abe107eaa0afdcb35f02/1455008783181/JRP%2B2016-2018%2BFull%2B160209.pdf. See also www.jrpsc.org/.

72. Yolanda Knell, "Desperate Syrian Refugees Return to War-Zone," BBC News, October 12, 2015 (www.bbc.com/news/world-middle-east-34504418). This is also raised by the UNHCR representative in Jordan, Andrew Harper, in "Relief Shortfall Forcing Syrian Refugees to Leave Jordan—UNHCR," *Venture Magazine,* Sep-

tember 20, 2015 (www.venturemagazine.me/2015/09/relief-short fall-forcing-syrian-refugees-to-leave-jordan-unhcr/).

73. Kemal Kirişci, interviews conducted at Al Quds Center for Political Studies, Amman, October 4, 2015, and the Hashemite Charity Organization, October 6, 2015.

74. Kemal Kirişci, interviews conducted with international nongovernmental organizations in Amman, October 4–6, 2015.

75. "Lebanon: Syrian Refugees Cost the Economy $4.5 Billion Every Year," *Fanack Chronicle*, June 23, 2015 (https://chronicle. fanack.com/lebanon/economy/lebanon-syrian-refugees-cost-the-economy-4-5-billion-every-year/).

76. Sam Jones and Kareem Shaheen, "Destitute Syrian Refugees in Jordan and Lebanon May Return to Warzone," *The Guardian*, September 11, 2015 (www.theguardian.com/global-development/2015/ sep/11/destitute-syrian-refugees-jordan-lebanon-may-return-to-warzone); see also "Lebanon: Looking Ahead in Times of Crisis," Oxfam Discussion Papers, December 2015, p. 19 (www.oxfam.org/ en/research/lebanon-looking-ahead-times-crisis).

77. Alsharabati and Nammour, *Survey on Perceptions of Syrian Refugees in Lebanon*, p. 4.

78. For a detailed discussion of the legal status of Syrian refugees in Turkey, see İçduygu, *Syrian Refugees in Turkey*.

79. Kirişci and Ferris, "Not Likely to Go Home."

80. Elizabeth Ferris and Kemal Kirişci, interviews with Turkish and UN officials in Istanbul, Ankara, and Gaziantep, June 11–19, 2015, and exchange of emails by Kirişci with refugee experts in Ankara in October 2015.

81. Ferris and Kirişci interviews, June 11–19, 2015.

82. Elizabeth Ferris and Kemal Kirişci, interviews with members of these NGOs in Istanbul, Şanlıurfa, and Gaziantep, June 11–18, 2015.

83. For example, see the programs and projects assisted by Support for Life (http://hayatadestek.org/en/projects/).

84. See Osman Bahadır Dinçer, Vittoria Federici, Elizabeth Ferris, Sema Karaca, Kemal Kirişci, and Elif Özmenek Çarmıklı, "Turkey and Syrian Refugees: Limits of Hospitality," Brookings-

USAK Reports, November 2013 (www.brookings.edu/~/media/ research/files/reports/2013/11/18-syria-turkey-refugees/turkey- and-syrian-refugees_the-limits-of-hospitality-(2014).pdf); and Kirişci and Ferris, "Not Likely to Go Home." The UNHCR has praised Turkey for running an "emergency response of a consis- tently high standard." See *2015 UNHCR Country Operations Profile —Turkey: Overview* (www.unhcr.org/pages/49e48e0fa7f.html).

85. "Struggling to Survive: Refugees from Syria in Turkey," Amnesty International, November 2014 (www.amnesty.org/en/ documents/EUR44/017/2014/en/). See also Ayça Söylemez, "Su- riyeli mülteciler Ankara'dan sürüldü [Syrian refugees expelled from Ankara]," *Bianet*, January 6, 2015 (http://bianet.org/bianet/ insan-haklari/161327-suriyeli-multeciler-ankara-dan-suruldu). On the effort to move Syrian refugees from the tourist resort of Antalya to refugee camps, see Sümeyye Ertekin, "Antalya'daki Suriyeliler gitmek istemiyor [Syrians in Antalya do not want to leave]," Al Jazeera Türk, December 22, 2014 (www.aljazeera.com. tr/al-jazeera-ozel/antalyadaki-suriyeliler-gitmek-istemiyor).

86. Melih Aslan, "Migrants Fleeing Syria Encounter a Life of Detention in Turkey"; and Human Rights Watch, "Turkey: Syri- ans Pushed Back at the Border," November 23, 2015 (www.hrw. org/news/2015/11/23/turkey-syrians-pushed-back-border); and Louisa Loveluck, "Turkey 'Turning away All Syrians Trying to Cross the Border,'" *Daily Telegraph*, November 23, 2015.

87. Kemal Kirişci, interview with Turkish academic with field experience, November 3, 2015.

88. On the notion of "guests," see Ayla Albayrak, "Turkey Denies Deporting Syrian," *Wall Street Journal,* March 28, 2013 (www.wsj. com/articles/SB10001424127887323361804578388402439423328); Ceylan Yeginsu, "Turkey Strengthens Rights of Syrian Refugees," *New York Times*, December 29, 2014 (www.nytimes.com/2014/12 /30/world/europe/turkey-strengthens-rights-of-syrian-refugees. html); Metin Çorabatır, "Suriye'de iç savaş ve insani güvenlik [Syrian civil war and human security]," *Milliyet*, September 18, 2013 (http://cadde.milliyet.com.tr/2012/07/24/YazarDetay/1765043 /suriye_de_ic_savas_ve_insani_guvenlik); and Oroub el-Abed, "The

Discourse of Guesthood: Forced Migrants in Jordan," in *Managing Muslim Mobilities*, edited by Anita Fabos and Riina Osotalo (New York: Palgrave MacMillan, 2014).

89. One report put the number of babies being born to Syrians families in Turkey at 100 a day; see Maysa Jalbout, "Partnering for a Better Future: Ensuring Educational Opportunity for All Syrian Refugee Children and Youth in Turkey," *A World at School Reports*, September 10, 2015, p. 18 (www.aworldatschool.org/page/-/uploads/Reports/Theirworld%20-%20Educational%20Opportunity%20for%20Syrian%20Children%20and%20Youth%20in%20Turkey%202015_09_10%20Release.pdf?nocdn=1). Another source gave the overall total born in Turkey at 60,000; see Ömür Budak, "Global Migrant Crisis Requires Global Effort," *Boston Globe*, November 14, 2015 (www.bostonglobe.com/opinion/2015/11/14/global-migrant-crisis-requires-global-effort/S4DVxSUm4NNJ9vWLh KVrpJ/story.html?event=event25). For Lebanon, the number of babies born was put at more than 50,000 in March 2015, most of whom were stateless; see Diana Al Rifai, "36,000 Newborn Syrians Stateless in Lebanon," Al Jazeera, May 11, 2015 (www.aljazeera.com/news/2015/05/150506060248502.html); and nearly 50,000 babies reportedly were been born in Jordan between 2011 and September 2015; see "48,600 Syrians Born in Jordan between 2011 and September 2015," *Jordan Times*, November 4, 2015 (www.jordantimes.com/news/local/48600-syrians-born-jordan-between-2011-september-2015%E2%80%99).

90. Kemal Kirişci and Raj Salooja, "Northern Exodus: How Turkey Can Integrate Syrian Refugees," *Foreign Affairs*, April 15, 2014 (www.foreignaffairs.com/articles/turkey/2014-04-15/northern-exodus).

91. Refugees/Migrants Emergency Response—Mediterranean, UNHCR (http://data.unhcr.org/mediterranean/regional.php), updated December 30, 2015.

92. Carli and Sekkarie, "Much Ado about Nothing?"; and Ximena V. Del Campo and Mathis Wagner, "The Impact of Syrian Refugees on the Turkish Labor Market," World Bank Working Paper, August 2015.

93. Erdoğan and Ünver, "Perspectives, Expectations and Suggestions of the Turkish Business Sector on Syrians in Turkey," pp. 43, 45.

94. Quoted in Mona Alami, "NGO Finds Work for Syrian Refugees in Turkey," *Al-Monitor*, August 7, 2015 (www.al-monitor.com/pulse/originals/2015/08/syrian-refugees-turkey-ngo-employ ment.html#ixzz3ktQWAXp4).

95. This development was mentioned frequently in interviews and discussed in some detail during a seminar at Hacettepe University, June 19, 2015. Also cited in European Commission, "Turkey, 2015 Report," Commission Staff Working Documents, November 20, 2015 (http://ec.europa.eu/enlargement/pdf/key_ documents/2015/20151110_report_turkey.pdf), p. 36.

96. Elizabeth Ferris and Kemal Kirişci, interview in Gaziantep, June 17, 2015. Similar observations have been cited in Orhan and Şenyücel Gündoğar, "Effects of the Syrian Refugees on Turkey," and Kanat and Üstün, "Turkey's Syrian Refugees: Toward Integration."

97. "ILO Joins UNHCR in Welcoming Turkey's Work Permit Offer to Syrian Refugees," *Hurriyet Daily News*, January 19, 2016 (www.hurriyetdailynews.com/ilo-joins-unhcr-in-welcoming-turkeys-work-permit-offer-to-syrian-refugees.aspx?pageID=238 &nID=94037&NewsCatID=341).

98. Erdoğan and Ünver, "Perspectives, Expectations and Suggestions of the Turkish Business Sector on Syrians in Turkey," p. 9.

99. Strochlic, "Jordan Squeezes Syrian Refugees."

100. Jordanian minister of labor quoted in Elisa Oddone, "Foreign, Local Workers at Odds in Jordan's Labor Market," Al-Monitor, June 3, 2015 (www.al-monitor.com/pulse/originals/2015/06/jordan-syria-refugee-crisis-unemployment.html#).

101. Stave and Hillesund, "Impact of Syrian Refugees on Jordanian Labor Market."

102. Mansur, "Let Them Work."

103. Oddone, "Foreign, Local Workers at Odds in Jordan's Labor Market."

104. Kemal Kirişci, interview with a representative of an international agency in Amman, October 6, 2015.

105. Exchange of emails with refugee experts in Amman, January 6, 2016.

106. "Lebanon: Syrian Refugees Cost the Economy $4.5 Billion," *Fanack Chronicle*; and International Monetary Fund, "Lebanon: Staff Report for the 2014 Article IV Consultation," IMF Country Report 14/237, July 2014 (www.imf.org/external/pubs/ft/scr/2014/cr14237.pdf).

107. United Nations Development Program and UNHCR, "Impact of Humanitarian Aid on Lebanese Economy," June 10, 2015 (http://reliefweb.int/report/lebanon/impact-humanitarian-aid-lebanese-economy).

108. "Assessment of the Impact of Syrian Refugees in Lebanon and Their Employment Profile," International Labor Organization, April 2014 (www.ilo.org/wcmsp5/groups/public/---arabstates/---ro-beirut/documents/genericdocument/wcms_240130.pdf).

109. Toufic Kasbar, "Syria War, Refugees Add to Lebanon's Economic Crisis," *Al-Monitor,* May 18, 2014 (www.al-monitor.com/pulse/politics/2014/05/lebanon-syria-conflict-refugees-economy-challenges-state.html#).

110. Zeena Zakharia, "Language and Vulnerability: How Educational Policies Exacerbate Inequalities in Higher Education," Middle East Institute, October 13, 2010, p. 20 (www.mei.edu/content/language-and-vulnerability-how-educational-policies-exacerbate-inequalities-higher-education).

111. Ibid. See also Human Rights Watch, "Preventing a Lost Generation: Turkey. When I Picture My Future, I See Nothing: Barriers to Education for Syrian Refugee Children in Turkey," November 2015 (www.hrw.org/sites/default/files/report_pdf/turkey1115_report-cover_web.pdf).

112. Elizabeth Ferris and Kemal Kirişci, interview with local officials in Gaziantep, June 17, 2015.

113. See figure on p. 10, "Partnering for a Better Future," *A World at School Report.* Human Rights Watch, "Preventing a Lost Generation," puts the number of Syrian children at school age at more than 700,000 with only an estimated quarter of children outside camps in schools, p. 22.

114. Remarks made during Elizabeth Ferris and Kemal

Kirişci's interview with local officials in Gaziantep, June 17, 2015. For similar observations by a Turkish official, see Human Rights Watch, "Preventing a Lost Generation," p. 17. And see Gordon Brown, "A Powerful Antidote to the Islamic State," *Washington Post,* November 29, 2015 (www.washingtonpost.com/opinions/antidote-to-isis-school-for-syrian-refugee-children/2015/11/29/4750d708-9232-11e5-8aa0-5d0946560a97_story.html).

115. Neils Harild, Asger Christensen, and Roger Zetter, *Sustainable Refugee Return: Triggers, Constraints and Lessons on Addressing the Development Challenges of Forced Displacement,* Global Program on Forced Displacement, World Bank Group, August 2015 (https://openknowledge.worldbank.org/bitstream/handle/10986/22751/Sustainable0re00forced0displacement.pdf?sequence=1&isAllowed=y).

116. Reuters, "Turkey Has Spent nearly $8 Billion Caring for 2.2 Million Syrian Refugees," *Huffington Post,* September 18, 2015 (www.huffingtonpost.com/entry/turkey-syrian-refugees_55fbd728e4b08820d9183073); Al-Kilani, "A Duty and a Burden on Jordan"; and "Lebanon Seeks $1B to Cope with Syria Crisis," *Daily Star,* March 31, 2015 (www.dailystar.com.lb/news/lebanon-news/2015/mar-31/292789-lebanon-seeks-1b-to-cope-with-syria-crisis.ashx).

117. Elena Ianchovichina and Maros Ivanic, "The Economic Impact of the Syrian War and the Spread of ISIS," World Bank Quick Notes Series, No. 140, January 2015 (http://siteresources.worldbank.org/INTMENA/Resources/QN140.pdf).

118. Financial Tracking Service of the UN Office for the Coordination of Humanitarian Affairs (UNOCHA), "Syria Response Plan, 2015," updated on January 5, 2016 (https://fts.unocha.org/pageloader.aspx?page=search-reporting_display&CQ=cq2601151910).

119. James Kanter and Anthony Higgins, "E.U. Offers Turkey 3 Billion Euros to Stem Migrant Flow," *New York Times,* November 29, 2015 (www.nytimes.com/2015/11/30/world/europe/eu-offers-turkey-3-billion-euros-to-stem-migrant-flow.html?emc=edit_ee_20151130&nl=todaysheadlines-europe&nlid=72815773&_r=0).

120. The funding rates for the Syrian Response Plan and the Syrian Regional Response and Resilience Plan for April 30, June 30, September 30, and November 30, 2015, were 10 percent and 10 percent; 19

percent and 23 percent; 31 percent and 36 percent, and 40 percent and 51 percent, respectively; see Financial Tracking Service of UNOCHA (https://fts.unocha.org/pageloader.aspx?page=special-syriancrisis).

121. "Syria Donors Conference 2016: Joint Announcement," UK Prime Minister's Office, Department for International Development and Foreign and Commonwealth Office press release (www.gov.uk/government/news/syria-donors-conference-2016-joint-announcement).

122. "G-20 Leaders' Communique Antalya Summit," Council of the European Council press releases and statements, November 16, 2015 (www.consilium.europa.eu/en/press/press-releases/2015/11/16-g20-summit-antalya-communique/).

123. "Resettlement and Other Forms of Legal Admission for Syrian Refugees," UNHCR, December 11, 2015 (www.unhcr.org/52b2febafc5.pdf).

124. See the data provided on UNHCR's website: http://data.unhcr.org/syrianrefugees/asylum.php

125. "Refugee Crisis: European Commission takes Decisive Action," European Commission press releases, September 9, 2015 (http://europa.eu/rapid/press-release_IP-15-5596_en.htm); and Ian Traynor and Patrick Kingsley, "EU Governments Push through Divisive Deal to Share 120,000 Refugees," *The Guardian*, September 22, 2015 (www.theguardian.com/world/2015/sep/22/eu-governments-divisive-quotas-deal-share-120000-refugees).

126. Dominic Casciani, "First of 20,000 Refugees Arrive in the UK," BBC News, September 22, 2015 (www.bbc.com/news/uk-34329459).

127. "France to Take in 24,000 Refugees over Next Two Years," *Middle East Monitor*, September 7, 2015 (www.middleeastmonitor.com/news/europe/20898-france-to-take-in-24000-refugees-over-next-two-years).

128. European Commission, "EU-Turkey Joint Action Plan," European Commission press releases, October 15, 2015 (http://europa.eu/rapid/press-release_MEMO-15-5860_en.htm).

129. European Commission, "Commission Recommendation of 15.12.2015 for a Voluntary Humanitarian Admission Scheme with Turkey," December 15, 2015 (http://ec.europa.eu/dgs/home-

affairs/what-we-do/policies/securing-eu-borders/legal-docu
ments/docs/commission_recommendation_for_a_voluntary_
humanitarian_admission_scheme_with_turkey_en.pdf).

130. European Commission, "Member States' Support to
Emergency Relocation Scheme," January 6, 2016 (http://ec.europa.
eu/dgs/home-affairs/what-we-do/policies/european-agenda-mig
ration/press-material/docs/state_of_play_-_relocation_en.pdf).

131. See Kate Connolly, Ian Traynor, and Constanze Letsch,
"Angela Merkel Backs Deal Offering Turkey up to 3bn Euros to
Tighten Its Borders," *The Guardian*, October 16, 2015 (www.the-
guardian.com/world/2015/oct/16/angela-merkel-eu-backs-aid-
deal-turkey-tighten-borders); "EU Delegation in Ankara to Look
for Common Ground over Refugee Crisis," *Today's Zaman*, October 14, 2015 (www.todayszaman.com/diplomacy_eu-delegation-in-
ankara-to-look-for-common-ground-over-refugee-crisis_401537.
html); and "Commissioner Hahn: EU to Seek Fresh Start with
Turkey," *Today's Zaman*, November 18, 2015 (www.todayszaman.
com/diplomacy_commissioner-hahn-eu-to-seek-fresh-start-with-
turkey_404603.html).

132. Zülfilar Doğan, "Some in Turkey Still Balk at the EU's 'In-
decent Proposal,'" *Al-Monitor*, November 18, 2015 (www.al-mon
itor.com/pulse/originals/2015/11/turkey-european-union-refugee-
proposal-creates-furor.html); Barın Kayaoğlu, "European Countries to Turkey: We Pay, You Keep Syrian Refugees," *Al-Monitor*,
September 2, 2015 (www.al-monitor.com/pulse/originals/2015/09/
turkey-syria-european-union-refugees-we-pay-you-keep-policy.
html#ixzz3wVk3YQAo); and Asli Aydintasbas, "Turkey: EU Partner or Buffer State?" European Council on Foreign Relations, December 2, 2015 (www.ecfr.eu/article/commentary_turkey_eu_partner_
or_buffer_state). For a detailed and critical analysis, in Turkish, of
the draft version of the plan, see Mustafa Kutlay and Öznur Akcalı,
"Mülteci Krizi ve Türkiye-AB İlişkilerinde Eksen Kayması Riski
[Refugee crisis and the risk of an axis-shift in Turkey-EU relations],"
USAK Analiz No. 29, 2015 (www.usak.org.tr/images_upload/files/
Book%201e.pdf).

133. Amnesty International, *Fears and Fences: Europe's Ap-*

proaches to Keeping Refugees at Bay (London: Amnesty International, November 2015), pp. 53–70. See more information on the report at www.amnesty.nl/sites/default/files/public/fear_and_fences_up dated_web_finalv2.pdf.

134. According to a survey conducted by the UNHCR among refugees in Greece, 37 percent indicated they came directly from Syria after transiting through a third country; see UNHCR, "Syrian Refugee Arrivals in Greece: Preliminary Questionnaire Findings April – September 2015," p. 9.

135. Ibid., p. 14.

136. "2015: Mehr Asylanträge in Deutschland als jemals zuvor [More asylum applications in Germany than ever before]," Bundesministerium des Innens [Ministry of the Interior], January 6, 2015. Germany received 1.1 million asylum-seekers during 2015, and almost half of them were Syrians (www.bmi.bund.de/SharedDocs/ Pressemitteilungen/DE/2016/01/asylantraege-dezember-2015. html).

137. Griff Witte, "Along the Migrant Trail: Pressure Grows to Close Europe's Open Borders," *Washington Post,* November 2, 2015 (www.washingtonpost.com/world/europe/along-the-migrant-trail-pressure-grows-to-close-europes-open-borders/2015/11/ 02/31fdfc30-7cc2-11e5-bfb6-65300a5ff562_story.html); Rosa Balfour, "Europe's Refugee Crisis and the Unraveling of the Union," *Transatlantic Take* (GMF blogs), September 16, 2015 (www.gmfus. org/blog/2015/09/16/europe%E2%80%99s-refugee-crisis-and-unravelling-union#sthash.LOmctNmh.dpuf); Editorial Board, "Europe Cannot Allow Xenophobia to Overpower Its Responses to Refugees," *Washington Post,* January 1, 2015 (www.washington post.com/opinions/europe-cannot-allow-its-tolerance-to-erode/2016/01/01/3a63ae7a-afed-11e5-9ab0-884d1cc4b33e_story. html); and Rudhain Mac Cormaic, "Selfishness on Refugees Has Brought EU to Its 'Knees,'" *Irish Times,* December 26, 2015 (www. irishtimes.com/news/world/selfishness-on-refugees-has-brought-eu-to-its-knees-1.2477702).

138. Abby Philip, "Governors Rush to Slam Door on Syrian Refugees," *Washington Post,* November 17, 2015 (www.washing

tonpost.com/news/post-politics/wp/2015/11/16/governors-rush-to-slam-door-on-syrian-refugees/).

139. Jie Zong and Jeanne Batalova, "Refugees and Asylees in the United States," Migration Policy Institute, October 28, 2015 (www.migrationpolicy.org/article/refugees-and-asylees-united-states).

140. Carol Morello, "3 Important Facts about How the U.S. Resettles Syrian Refugees," *Washington Post,* November 17, 2015 (www.washingtonpost.com/news/worldviews/wp/2015/11/17/3-important-facts-about-how-the-u-s-resettles-syrian-refugees/).

141. For the report, in Turkish, see "Türkiye'deki Suriyeli mülteci sayısı 70 bine yaklaştı [The number of Syrian refugees in Turkey is closing in on 70,000]," BBC Türkçe, August 20, 2012 (www.bbc.com/turkce/haberler/2012/08/120820_turkey_syria.shtml); and Burcu Çalık, "Mülteci sayısı psikolojik sınırı aştı [The number of refugees has crossed the psychological threshold]," *Sabah*, October 16, 2012 (www.sabah.com.tr/gundem/2012/10/16/multeci-sayisi-psikolojik-siniri-asti).

142. Anne Barnard, Michael R. Gordon, and Eric Schmitt, "Turkey and U.S. Plan to Create Syria 'Safe Zone' Free of ISIS," *New York Times,* July 27, 2015 (www.nytimes.com/2015/07/28/world/middleeast/turkey-and-us-agree-on-plan-to-clear-isis-from-strip-of-northern-syria.html?_r=1); and "Davutoglu Calls for Safe Zone," *Middle East Monitor,* July 28, 2015 (www.middleeastmonitor.com/news/middle-east/20073-davutoglu-calls-for-safe-zone-in-syria).

143. "Syrian Safe Zone: US Relents to Turkish Demands after Border Crisis Grows," *The Guardian*, July 27, 2015 (www.the-guardian.com/world/2015/jul/27/syrian-safe-zone-us-relents-to-turkish-demands-border-crisis-kurd-uk-military); Jeremy Shapiro, "Turkey's Shift on ISIS Is a Mark of U.S. Success," *Financial Times*, August 24, 2015 (www.ft.com/intl/cms/s/0/d41e1de4-4683-11e5-af2f-4d6e0e5eda22.html); and "U.S. Denies Reaching Agreement with Turkey on Syria 'Safe Zone,'" *Hürriyet Daily News*, August 12, 2015 (www.hurriyetdailynews.com/us-denies-reaching-agreement-with-turkey-on-syria-safe-zone.aspx?PageID=238&NID=86810&NewsCatID=352).

144. "Press Conference by President Obama—Antalya, Turkey," Archives of the White House Press Office, November 16, 2015 (www.whitehouse.gov/the-press-office/2015/11/16/press-confer ence-president-obama-antalya-turkey). For President Erdogan's speech, in Turkish, after the G-20 summit in November 2015, see Recep Tayyip Erdoğan, "G20 Antalya Liderler Zirvesi Sonunda Basın Toplantısında Yaptıkları Konuşması [Speech at the press conference following G20 Antalya leaders summit]," November 16, 2015 (www.tccb.gov.tr/konusmalar/353/36000/g-20-antalya -liderler-zirvesi-sonunda-basin-toplantisinda-yaptiklari-konus ma.html).

145. Fehim Taştekin, "Davutoglu Proposes Refugee 'Container City,'" *Al-Monitor*, September 30, 2015 (www.al-monitor.com/ pulse/originals/2015/09/turkey-syria-assad-boutique-state-refugees-container-state.html).

146. Soner Cagaptay and James F. Jeffrey, "How Will the Turkey-Russia Crisis Affect Ankara's NATO Ties?," *Policywatch* 2530, Washington Institute for Near East Policy, December 9, 2015 (www. washingtoninstitute.org/policy-analysis/view/how-will-the-turkey-russia-crisis-affect-ankaras-nato-ties); and Fredrik Wesslau, "Why Is Russia Still Turning up the Heat on Turkey?," *EFCR Commentary*, December 2, 2015 (www.ecfr.eu/article/commentary_why_is_russia_still_turning_up_the_heat_on_turkey5040).

CHAPTER 3

1. See the text of United Nations General Assembly Resolution 46/182 of December 19, 1991 (www.un.org/documents/ga/res/46/ a46r182.htm).

2. United Nations, OCHA, *Guiding Principles on Internal Displacement*, 1998 (www.brookings.edu/~/media/Projects/idp/ GPEnglish.pdf).

3. World Summit Outcome, October 2005, p. 28 (http://dac-cessdds.un.org/doc/UNDOC/GEN/N05/487/60/PDF/N0548760. pdf?OpenElement).

4. For a sampling of acknowledgements of this fact by the principal architects of Responsibility to Protect and a discussion of the symmetry of the two conceptual frameworks, see Erin Mooney, "Something Old, Something New: The Protection Potential of a Marriage of Concepts between R2P and IDP Protection," *Global Responsibility to Protect* 2, no 1 (2010): 60–85 (see especially pp. 72–77). See also Gareth Evans, *The Responsibility to Protect: Ending Mass Atrocity Crimes Once and for All* (Brookings, 2008), pp. 36–37; and Roberta Cohen, "Reconciling R2P with IDP Protection," in *Protecting the Displaced: Deepening the Responsibility to Protect,* edited by Sara E. Davies and Luke Glanville (Leiden, The Netherlands: Martinus Nijhoff, 2010), p. 35.

5. Office of the High Commissioner for Human Rights, "United Nations Commission of Inquiry on Syria: Impunity Prevails as Little Progress Is Made towards Securing Peace and Justice for Syrians," February 20, 2015 (www.ohchr.org/EN/NewsEvents/Pages/DisplayNews.aspx?NewsID=15594&LangID=E#sthash.Cy7ZFXzQ.dpuf). The report also notes that ISIS and the al-Qaeda–affiliated al-Nusra Front are dealing brutally with civilians and minorities and that ISIS is also escalating its terror tactics against the Syrian population, including public executions and mutilations.

6. Guillaume Charron and Emilie Arnaud, "A Full-Scale Displacement and Humanitarian Crisis with no Solutions in Sight," Internal Displacement Monitoring Centre, July 31, 2012 (www.internal-displacement.org/middle-east-and-north-africa/syria/2012/a-full-scale-displacement-and-humanitarian-crisis-with-no-solutions-in-sight).

7. Note that details are not provided by OCHA about these figures. And there are some contradictions. Even as the October 2015 figures are a decrease, OCHA's *Humanitarian Bulletin Syria* No. 2, June 2015, notes that more than 540,000 people were newly displaced in the first four months of 2015. This suggests that either over 1.5 million Syrian IDPs left the country or returned to their homes (and thus were not considered IDPs) or that the October 2014 figure of 7.6 million was inflated. See www.humanitarianresponse.info/en/operations/whole-of-syria/document/humanitarian-syria-issue-2-june-2015.

8. See OCHA's webpage on the Syrian Arab Republic (www. unocha.org/syria).

9. OCHA, "Estimated People in Need and Number of IDPs per Governorate" (http://reliefweb.int/sites/reliefweb.int/files/resources/estimated_pin_idps_per_governorate_151105.pdf).

10. OCHA's webpage on the Syrian Arab Republic.

11. Internal Displacement Monitoring Centre and Norwegian Refugee Center, *Global Overview 2015: People Internally Displaced by Conflict and Violence*, May 2015, p. 39 (internal-displacement. org/assets/library/Media/201505-Global-Overview-2015/2015 0506-global-overview-2015-en.pdf).

12. Ibid.

13. U.S. Agency for International Development, "Syria Complex Emergency Fact Sheet #8," September 21, 2015 (www.usaid. gov/crisis/syria/fy15/fs08).

14. Interview with Elizabeth Ferris, June 4, 2013.

15. Internal Displacement Monitoring Centre and Norwegian Refugee Center, *Global Overview 2015,* p. 40.

16. UN General Assembly, "Report of the Special Rapporteur on the human rights of internally displaced persons," A/67, July 15, 2013 (www.ohchr.org/Documents/Issues/IDPersons/A_67_931Syria_ report.pdf).

17. Ibid.

18. UNHCR, "Syria Regional Refugee Response" (http://data. unhcr.org/syrianrefugees/regional.php).

19. UN Human Rights Council, "Report of the Independent International Commission of Inquiry on the Syrian Arab Republic," A/ HRC/30/48, August 13, 2015, p. 12 (www.ohchr.org/EN/HRBodies/ HRC/RegularSessions/Session28/Documents/A.HRC.28.69_E.doc).

20. UN General Assembly, "Report of the Special Rapporteur," July 15, 2013.

21. OCHA, *Humanitarian Bulletin Syria* No. 2, June 2015.

22. Chaloka Beyani, "Statement by the Special Rapporteur on the Human Rights of Internally Displaced Persons on the conclusion of his official visit to the Syrian Arab Republic—May 16–19, 2015," May 2015 (www.ohchr.org/en/NewsEvents/Pages/Display News.aspx?NewsID=16008&LangID=E).

23. Global Protection Cluster, *War in Syria: The Hidden Costs of Gender-Based Violence*, April 2013, pp. 1–2. Also see UN Human Rights Council, "Report of the Independent International Commission of Inquiry on the Syrian Arab Republic," A/HRC/30/48, August 13, 2015.

24. On April 30, 2013, artillery bombs reportedly hit a makeshift IDP camp near Bab Al-Hawa on the Turkish border, resulting in at least fifty persons wounded and five killed, UN Department of Safety and Security information, April 30, 2013. See also Khaled Yacoub Oweis, "Syrian Air Strike on Turkish Border Kills at Least Five," Reuters, April 30, 2013 (www.reuters.com/article/2013/04/30/us-syria-crisis-turkey-idUSBRE93T0QQ20130430).

25. UN General Assembly and UN Security Council, "Children and Armed Conflict: Report of the Secretary-General," A/67/845–S/2013/245, May 15, 2013, paras 77, 151–60 (http://daccess-dds-ny.un.org/doc/UNDOC/GEN/N13/311/67/PDF/N1331167.pdf?OpenElement).

26. Beyani, "Statement by the Special Rapporteur on the Human Rights of Internally Displaced Persons."

27. UN General Assembly, "Report of the Special Rapporteur," July 15, 2013, p. 17.

28. Ibid.

29. Ibid., p. 18.

30. See UNRWA's website on the Syria Crisis (www.unrwa.org/syria-crisis#Syria-Crisis-and-Palestine-refugees).

31. Jonathan Steele, "How Yarmouk Refugee Camp Became the Worst Place in Syria," *The Guardian*, March 5, 2015 (www.theguardian.com/news/2015/mar/05/how-yarmouk-refugee-camp-became-worst-place-syria); and "Typhoid Outbreak Grips Syria's Yarmouk," Al Jazeera, September 23, 2015 (www.aljazeera.com/news/2015/09/typhoid-outbreak-grips-syria-yarmouk-150923145914286.html).

32. Frederick Pleitgen, "Inside Syria: The Wasteland of Yarmouk That Sums up Four Years of Civil War," CNN, August 20, 2015 (http://edition.cnn.com/2015/08/13/middleeast/syria-yarmouk-front-line/). Also see Michelle Nichols, "UN Security Council Mulls How to Help Yarmouk's Civilians," Reuters, April 6, 2015 (www.

reuters.com/article/2015/04/06/us-mideast-crisis-syria-yarmouk-idUSKBN0MX1B620150406#82hCTdGuF4MdwMk8.97); Jonathan Steele, "How Yarmouk Refugee Camp Became the Worst Place in Syria"; and "Typhoid Outbreak Grips Syria's Yarmouk," Al Jazeera.

33. UNHCR Statistical Database at http://data.un.org/Data.aspx?d=UNHCR&f=indID%3AType-Ref.

34. Elizabeth Ferris, "Remembering Iraq's Displaced," Brookings, March 18, 2013 (www.brookings.edu/research/articles/2013/03/18-iraq-displaced-ferris).

35. UN Human Rights Council, "Report of the Independent International Commission of Inquiry on the Syrian Arab Republic."

36. Bob Bowker, "Syria: World Dithers as New Refugee Crisis Looms," Lowy Interpreter, July 15, 2015 (www.lowyinterpreter.org/post/2015/07/15/Syria-World-dithers-as-new-refugee-crisis-looms.aspx); and Charlotte McDonald-Gibson, "Syrians Flee Their Homes amid Fears of Ethnic Cleansing," *The Independent*, February 17, 2012 (www.independent.co.uk/news/world/middle-east/syrians-flee-their-homes-amid-fears-of-ethnic-cleansing-7079802.html).

37. "UNHCR Ramps up Registration of Syrian Refugees in Lebanon," May 27, 2013 (www.unhcr.org/51a35bdd9.html).

38. Kemal Kirişci, interview with a member of parliament from the Republican People's Party, January 2014.

39. Constanze Letsch, "Syrian Conflict brings Sectarian Tensions to Turkey's Tolerant Hatay Province," *The Guardian*, September 3, 2013 (www.theguardian.com/world/2013/sep/03/syria-crisis-threatens-turkish-tolerance).

40. Dorian Jones, "Seeking Safety: Syria's Christians flee to Turkey," Voice of America, December 17, 2013 (www.voanews.com/content/seeking-safety-syrias-christian-flee-to-turkey/1812413.html).

41. Jonathan Burch, "Turkey Building Refugee Camps for Syrian Christians, Kurds," Reuters, April 10, 2013 (www.reuters.com/article/2013/04/10/us-syria-crisis-turkey-minorities-idUSBRE9390MA20130410).

42. Jones, "Seeking Safety."

43. Nil Koksal, "Syrian Christians Fleeing ISIS Find Shelter

in Turkey," CBC News, April 3, 2015 (www.cbc.ca/news/world/syrian-christians-fleeing-isis-find-shelter-in-turkey-1.3020582).

44. "Bishop Accuses Turkey over Syrian Christians," *Hurriyet DailyNews,* February 25, 2015 (www.hurriyetdailynews.com/bishop-accuses-turkey-over-syrian-christians-.aspx?PageID=238&NID=78846&NewsCatID=352).

45. Anadolu Agency, "Syria's Armenians Find Safe Haven in Turkey," *Daily Sabah,* August 7, 2015 (www.dailysabah.com/nation/2015/08/08/syrias-armenians-find-safe-haven-in-turkey.

46. "Syria's Armenians Look to Ancient Homeland for Safety," BBC News, September 10, 2015 (www.bbc.com/news/world-europe-34210854).

47. Liana Aghajanian, "Long-Persecuted Yazidis Find Second Homeland in Armenia," Al Jazeera America, September 24, 2014 (http://america.aljazeera.com/articles/2014/9/24/a-second-homeland.html).

48. Loveday Morris, "Syrian Armenians, Who Had Been Insulated from War, Forced to Flee after Rebel Offensive," *Washington Post,* April 2, 2014 (www.washingtonpost.com/world/middle_east/until-last-month-this-ancestral-home-of-syrian-armenians-had-been-insulated-from-war/2014/04/02/84a97180-5224-40fc-bcdf-6920aae3a7ab_story.html).

49. European Roma Rights Centre, *The Situation of Dom Refugees from Syria in Turkey,* September 23, 2015 (www.errc.org/article/nowhere-to-turn-the-situation-of-dom-refugees-from-syria-in-turkey/4419).

50. Carsten Wieland, Adam Almqvist, and Helena Nassif, *The Syrian Uprising: Dynamics of an Insurgency* (University of St. Andrews, Centre for Syrian Studies, 2013), p. 35.

51. International Crisis Group, "Syria's Kurds: A Struggle within a Struggle," *ICG Middle East Report* 136, January 2, 2013, p. i (www.crisisgroup.org/en/regions/middle-east-north-africa/egypt-syria-lebanon/syria/136-syrias-kurds-a-struggle-within-a-struggle.aspx).

52. Cengiz Güneş and Robert Lowe, "The Impact of the Syrian War on Kurdish Politics across the Middle East," Chatham House Research Paper, July 2015, Chatham House, London (www

.chathamhouse.org/sites/files/chathamhouse/field/field_docume nt/20150723SyriaKurdsGunesLowe.pdf).

53. International Crisis Group, "Syria's Kurds," p. ii.

54. "PYD Declaration of New Syrian Canton Raises Displacement Fears among Population," *Daily Sabah*, October 21, 2015 (www.dailysabah.com/mideast/2015/10/21/pyd-declaration-of-new-syria-canton-raises-displacement-fears-among-population).

55. Tim Arango and Eric Schmitt, "Turkey Uneasy as US Support of Syrian Kurds Grows," *New York Times*, June 29, 2015 (www.nytimes.com/2015/06/30/world/middleeast/turkey-uneasy-as-us-support-of-syrian-kurds-grows.html?_r=0).

56. "Islamic State Conflict: Syrian Kurds 'Seize Tal Abyad,'" BBC News, June 15, 2015 (www.bbc.com/news/world-middle-east-3313 2809).

57. Joseph Micallef, "Turkey and the Kurdish Corridor: Why the Islamic State Survives," *Huffington Post*, August 16, 2015 (www.huffingtonpost.com/joseph-v-micallef/turkey-and-the-kurdish-co_b_7994540.html?ncid=txtlnkusaolp00000592).

58. UNHCR, "Syrian Regional Refugee Response: Iraq" (http://data.unhcr.org/syrianrefugees/country.php?id=103).

59. Samer Muscati, "Syrian Kurds Flee to Iraqi Safe Haven," Human Rights Watch, May 14, 2012 (www.hrw.org/news/2012/05/14/syrian-kurds-fleeing-iraqi-safe-haven).

60. International Organization for Migration, *Iraq: The Impact of the Syrian Crisis* (Geneva: IOM, September 2013), p. 24 (http://data.unhcr.org/syrianrefugees/download.php?id=2947).

61. UNHCR, "Growing Number of Syrian Refugees from Kobane Seek Safety in Northern Iraq, Eastern Syria," October 10, 2014 (www.unhcr.org/5437ad67f95.html).

62. Kemal Kirişci and Elizabeth Ferris, "Not Likely to Go Home: Syrian Refugees and the Challenges to Turkey—and the International Community," Turkey Project Policy Paper No. 7, Brookings, September 2015 (www.brookings.edu/research/files/papers/2015/09/syrian-refugee-international-challenges-ferris-kirisci/).

63. "Suruc Massacre: Turkey Suicide Bombing Suspect Identi-

fied," BBC News, July 21, 2015 (www.bbc.com/news/world-europe-33606291).

64. "Kurdish Militants Say Kill Two Turkish Police to Avenge Islamic State Bombing," Reuters, July 22, 2015 (http://uk.reuters.com/article/2015/07/22/uk-mideast-crisis-turkey-idUKKCN0PW0PA20150722).

65. Tom Wyke, "Turkey Launches Deadly Airstrikes on ISIS and PKK Bases as Kurds Threaten to Tear up Ceasefire Agreement," *Daily Mail*, July 25, 2015 (www.dailymail.co.uk/news/article-3174295/Fighting-Turkey-launches-deadly-airstrikes-ISIS-PKK-bases-Kurds-threaten-tear-ceasefire-agreement.html).

66. International Crisis Group, "Syria's Kurds," p. iii.

67. The exception is Israel, which has kept its borders closed to Syrians. But even in Israel, there are reports of Syrians being allowed to enter the country for medical treatment; see Isabel Kershner, "Across Forbidden Border, Doctors in Israel Quietly Tend to Syria's Wounded," *New York Times*, August 5, 2013 (www.nytimes.com/2013/08/06/world/middleeast/across-forbidden-border-doctors-in-israel-quietly-tend-to-syrias-wounded.html?pagewanted=all&_r=0).

68. Ben Parker, *Humanitarianism Besieged*, Humanitarian Practice Network, November 2013 (http://odihpn.org/magazine/humanitarianism-besieged/).

69. Ibid.

70. Syria Needs Analysis Project, "Regional Analysis Syria," *Regional Analysis of the Syria Conflict (RAS)*, July 3, 2013, p. 6 (http://reliefweb.int/sites/reliefweb.int/files/resources/overview_july_2014.pdf).

71. Daryl Grisgraber and Sarnata Reynolds, "Aid inside Syria: A Step in the Right Direction?" Refugees International Field Report, May 12, 2015, p. 3 (http://static1.squarespace.com/static/506c8ea1e4b01d9450dd53f5/t/5604770ce4b0be7e3d4c33be/1443133196237/150511_syria_local_aid.pdf).

72. Tom Esslemont, "Syria Red Crescent Boss Says Won't Give up in the Face of Colleague Deaths, Bloodshed," Reuters, June 16, 2015 (www.reuters.com/article/2015/06/16/us-syria-red-crescent-idUSKBN0OW2D020150616#eA4zs8MKIs80pgVC.97).

73. Parker, *Humanitarianism Besieged.*

74. Fourteen others had been approved in principle and planning was proceeding, three areas can be reached through regular UN channels, five were put on hold by the UN because of security concerns, six requests lapsed, and fifteen requests were pending approval. OCHA, *Humanitarian Bulletin Syria* No. 1, May 7, 2015 (www.humanitarianresponse.info/en/operations/whole-of-syria/document/whole-syria-humanitarian-bulletin-issue-no-1). Note that this refers to interagency convoys, while single-agency deliveries across conflict lines may also have been taking place.

75. See, for example, Valerie Amos, "Security Council Briefing on Syria," April 18, 2013, p. 3 (https://docs.unocha.org/sites/dms/Documents/USG%20Amos%20Security%20Council%20on%20Syria%2018%20April%202013%20CAD.pdf).

76. OCHA, *Humanitarian Bulletin Syria* No. 2, June 2015.

77. OCHA, *Humanitarian Bulletin Syria* No. 1, May 7, 2015.

78. World Food Program USA, "Syria Situation Update," September 2015 (http://wfpusa.org/fact-sheets/syria-situation-update).

79. Associated Press, "Lack of Funds: World Food Program drops aid to one third of Syrian refugees," *The Guardian,* September 4, 2015 (www.theguardian.com/world/2015/sep/05/lack-of-funds-world-food-programme-drops-aid-to-one-third-of-syrian-refugees).

80. Parker, *Humanitarianism Besieged.*

81. See OCHA, "Overview: Whole of Syria," Humanitarian Response (www.humanitarianresponse.info/en/operations/whole-of-syria).

82. Ibid.

83. UN Security Council, "Report of the Secretary-General on the implementation of Security Council Resolutions, 2139 (2014), 2165 (2014) and 2191 (2014)," August 20, 2015 (www.un.org/en/ga/search/view_doc.asp?symbol=S/2015/651), and June 23, 2015 (www.un.org/en/ga/search/view_doc.asp?symbol=S/2015/468).

84. Ibid.

85. Syrian American Medical Society, "Slow Death: Life and Death in Syrian Communities under Siege," Syrian American Medical Society Report, March 2015 (http://syriaundersiege.org/wp-content/uploads/2015/03/For-web-_REPORT.pdf).

86. UN Human Rights Council, "Report of the Independent International Commission of Inquiry on the Syrian Arab Republic," A/HRC/30/48, August 13, 2015, p. 15.

87. ACAPS, Strategic Needs Analysis Project, "Regional Analysis Syria Brief," November 1–December 7, 2014, p. 5 (www.acaps. org/en/pages/syria-snap-project).

88. Amnesty International, "Left to Die under Siege: War Crimes and Human Rights Abuses in Eastern Ghouta, Syria," August 2015, p. 7 (www.amnesty.org/en/documents/mde24/2079/2015/en/).

89. Ibid., p. 12.

90. Ibid., p. 7.

91. UN Security Council, *Implementation of Security Council Resolutions*, August 20, 2015, and June 23, 2015.

92. Syrian American Medical Society, "Slow Death," p. 22.

93. Ibid., pp. 24–26.

94. Michelle Nichols, "UN Security Council authorizes crossborder aid access in Syria," Reuters, July 14, 2014 (www.reuters. com/article/2014/07/14/us-syria-crisis-un-aid-idUSKBN0FJ1Z32 0140714#HYfcOiRbwbOfuZrs.97).

95. Michelle Nichols, "U.N. Approved Cross Border Aid Helps 600,000 Syrians in Six Months," Reuters, January 22, 2015 (www. reuters.com/article/2015/01/22/us-mideast-crisis-syria-un-idUSK BN0KV2V120150122#tiodEUFZ7tCzKPsq.97).

96. "Aid Agencies Give UN a 'Failing Grade' on Syria," Al Jazeera America, March 12, 2015 (http://america.aljazeera.com/ articles/2015/3/12/aid-groups-give-un-failing-grade-on-syria. html). Also see Grisgraber and Reynolds, "Aid inside Syria," p. 1.

97. Robin Wright, "A Turkish City on the Frontier of Syria's War," *New Yorker*, December 8, 2014 (www.newyorker.com/ magazine/2014/12/08/vortex).

98. Adam Withnall, "Battle for Azaz: ISIS Threatens Yet another City as Fighting Reaches Crucial Turkish Border Crossing," *The Independent*, June 1, 2015 (www.independent.co.uk/news/world /middle-east/battle-for-azaz-isis-threatens-yet-another-city-as-fighting-reaches-crucial-turkey-border-crossing-10289708 .html).

99. U.S. Agency for International Development, "Syria Complex Emergency," Fact Sheet No. 8, September 21, 2015 (www.usaid .gov/crisis/syria/fy15/fs08).

100. Grisgraber and Reynolds, "Aid inside Syria," p. 1.

101. Ibid., p. 4.

102. Ibid., p. 6.

103. Ibid., pp. 8–9.

104. Ibid., p. 5.

105. Ibid., p. 6. Also note that the tension inherent in international nongovernmental organizations subcontracting work to local NGOs is also present in refugee situations where local NGOs complain that much of the money is taken by the international agencies for administrative costs rather than supporting the local NGO or being given to the beneficiaries.

106. Ibid., p. 10.

107. We are indebted to Louise Virenfeldt, former intern at the Brookings IDP Project, for this term.

108. Taylor Seyboldt, *Humanitarian Intervention: The Conditions for Success and Failure* (Stockholm: Stockholm International Peace Research Institute, 2003) (http://books.sipri.org/files/books/ SIPRI08Seybolt.pdf).

109. Phil Orchard, "Revisiting Humanitarian Safe Areas for Civilian Protection," *Global Governance* 20, no. 1 (2014): 55–75 (see especially pp. 56–64).

110. International Committee of the Red Cross and InterAction, "Outcome Report: Trapped in Conflict: Evaluating Scenarios to Assist At-Risk Civilians," April 24, 2015, p. 7 (www.interaction. org/document/trapped-conflict-roundtable-outcome-report). Also see Bill Frelick, "Safe Zones in Name Only," *Huffington Post*, August 21, 2015 (www.huffingtonpost.com/bill-frelick/safe-zones-in-name-only_b_8021010.html).

111. International Committee of the Red Cross and InterAction, "Outcome Report," pp. 9–10.

112. Ibid., p. 11.

113. Ibid., pp. 10–11.

114. See, for example, Michael O'Hanlon, "Deconstructing the

Syria Nightmare," *National Interest,* October 22, 2015 (www. nationalinterest.org/feature/deconstructing-the-syria-nightmare-14108?page=2); Mark Mazzetti and Peter Baker, "U.S. Is Debating Ways to Shield Syrian Civilians," *New York Times,* October 22, 2015 (www.nytimes.com/2015/10/23/world/middleeast/us-considering-ways-to-shield-syrian-civilians.html?smid=nytcore-iphone-share&smprod=nytcore-iphone&_r=0); Asli Aydintasbas, "Proxy War Worsens between Russia and Turkey," *ECFR Commentary,* November 25, 2015 (www.ecfr.eu/article/commentary_proxy_war_worsens_between_russia_and_turkey5031); Dania Akkad, "Russia's Syria Intervention Renews Push for a Safe-Zone," *Middle East Eye* (www.middleeasteye.net/news/russias-syrian-intervetion-rein vigorates-calls-safe-zone-1464848813); and Kristina Wong, "State: 'No Viable Option' for Safe Zones in Syria," *The Hill,* April 11, 2015 (http://thehill.com/policy/defense/259183-state-depart ment-officials-no-viable-option-on-the-table-for-safe-zones-in).

115. Diane Paul, "Time to Act: The Argument for No-Fly Zones and Safe Areas to Protect Civilians in Syria," *Professionals in Humanitarian Assistance and Protection,* June 11, 2013 (https:// phap.org/articles/time-act-argument-no-fly-zones-and-safe-areas-protect-civilians-syria).

116. Nicholas Henin, "Bombs Won't Defeat Terrorists," Handelsblatt, December 8, 2015 (https://global.handelsblatt.com/ edition/323/ressort/opinion/article/bombs-wont-defeat-terrorists?ref=MzQ0NzI0&contact_id).

117. O'Hanlon, "Deconstructing the Syria Nightmare."

118. Philip Gordon, James Dobbins, and Jeff Martini, "A Realistic Peace Plan for Syria Needs to Begin with an Immediate Ceasefire," *Washington Post,* December 17, 2015 (www.washing-tonpost.com/opinions/a-realistic-peace-plan-for-syria/2015 /12/17/1a004eca-a414-11e5-ad3f-991ce3374e23_story.html).

119. James Dettmar, "It's High Time the US Imposed a No-Fly Zone over Northern Syria," *Daily Beast,* May 4, 2015 (www. thedailybeast.com/articles/2015/05/04/it-s-high-time-the-u-s-imposed-a-no-fly-zone-over-northern-syria.html).

120. "Remarks by Senator John McCain on Syria at the American Enterprise Institute, June 18, 2012 (www.mccain.senate.

gov/public/index.cfm/speeches?ID=0090a3b8-a9d9-5ca5-382b-bd77b044b049).

121. Anne Gearan, "Clinton Joins Some Republicans in Breaking with Obama on Syria No-Fly Zone," *Washington Post,* October 2, 2015 (www.washingtonpost.com/news/post-politics/wp/2015/10/02/in-break-with-white-house-clinton-advocates-syria-no-fly-zone/). Also see Pam Key, "Trump: I Will Build a 'Big, Beautiful Safe Zone' in Syria for Refugees," Breitbart, November 18, 2015 (www.breitbart.com/video/2015/11/17/trump-i-will-build-a-big-beautiful-safe-zone-in-syria-for-refugees/).

122. Fredrik Wesslau, "Why Is Russia Still Turning up the Heat on Turkey?," *ECFR Commentary,* December 2, 2015 (www.ecfr.eu/article/commentary_why_is_russia_still_turning_up_the_heat_on_turkey5040); and Aydintasbas, "The Proxy-War Worsens between Russia and Turkey."

123. Liz Sly, "Russian Airstrikes Disrupt Aid Delivery to Syria," *Washington Post,* December 14, 2015 (www.washingtonpost.com/world/middle_east/russian-airstrikes-force-a-halt-to-aid-in-syria-triggering-a-new-crisis/2015/12/14/cebc4b66-9f87-11e5-9ad2-568d814bbf3b_story.html).

124. Lucinda Smith, "Russia Jet 'May Have Been Preparing to Strike Refugee Camp,'" *The Times,* November 26, 2015 (www.theaustralian.com.au/news/world/russia-jet-may-have-been-preparing-to-strike-refugee-camp/news-story/620374807bc82c9f7851483b34a7797a?sv=9efb6b9397543b3d84d2e5c81a57d999). Also see Amnesty International, "Russia's Shameful Failure to Acknowledge Civilian Killings," December 23, 2015 (www.amnesty.org/en/latest/news/2015/12/syria-russias-shameful-failure-to-acknowledge-civilian-killings/).

125. Wesslau, "Why Is Russia Still Turning up the Heat on Turkey?"

126. Vladimir Putin, Presidential Address to the Federal Assembly, December 3, 2015 (http://en.kremlin.ru/events/president/news/50864).

127. Wesslau, "Why Is Russia Still Turning up the Heat on Turkey?"

NOTES TO CHAPTER 4

1. United Nations Charter, "Preamble" (www.un.org/en/sec tions/un-charter/preamble/index.html).

2. "Security Council Unanimously Adopts Resolution 2254 (2015) Endorsing Road Map for Peace Process in Syria, Setting Timetable for Talks," UN meetings coverage and press releases, December 18, 2015 (www.un.org/press/en/2015/sc12171.doc.htm).

3. For an overview of these initiatives, see documents available at Global Policy Forum (www.globalpolicy.org/security-council/ security-council-reform.html).

4. See, for example, "Final Communiqué of the Open-Ended Emergency Meeting on the Syrian Refugee Crisis," adopted September 13, 2015 (www.oic-oci.org/oicv2/topic/?t_id=10450&t_ ref=4124&lan=en). Also see "OIC Blames Assad Regime for Syria's Humanitarian Crisis," *Middle East Monitor*, September 14, 2015 (www.middleeastmonitor.com/news/middle-east/21062-oic-blames-assad-regime-for-syrias-humanitarian-crisis). And see Khalaf Ahmad Al Habloor, "Syria Refugee Crisis: Arab League's Inaction Is Shameful," Al Arabiya, September 21, 2015 (http://english.alar-abiya.net/en/views/news/middle-east/2015/09/21/Syria-refugee-crisis-Arab-League-s-inaction-is-shameful.html).

5. "Why the Schengen Agreement Might Be under Threat," *The Economist*, August 24, 2015 (www.economist.com/blogs/econo mist-explains/2015/08/economist-explains-18).

6. Note, for example, the imposition of border controls by Scandinavian governments in early January 2015. David Crouch, "Sweden and Denmark Crack down on Refugees at Border," *The Guardian*, January 3, 2015 (www.theguardian.com/world/2016/ jan/03/sweden-to-impose-id-checks-on-travellers-from-denmark). See also "Europe Cannot Allow Xenophobia to Over-power Its Response to Refugees," *Washington Post*, January 1, 2016 (www.washingtonpost.com/opinions/europe-cannot-allow-its-tolerance-to-erode/2016/01/01/3a63ae7a-afed-11e5-9ab0-884d1cc4b33e_story.html).

7. U.S. Institute for Peace, "Refugee Crisis Illustrates Need to Redouble Middle East Efforts, Experts Say," September 18, 2015

(www.usip.org/publications/2015/09/18/refugee-crisis-illustrates-need-redouble-middle-east-efforts-experts-say).

8. Homa Haider, *Refugee, IDP and Host Community Radicalization*, GSDRC Helpdesk Research Report 1162, GSDRC, University of Birmingham, Birmingham, UK, 2014, p. 3.

9. Krishnadev Calamur, "How Much Does It Cost to Settle a Syrian Refugee in the US?," *The Atlantic,* September 14, 2015 (www.theatlantic.com/notes/all/2015/08/the-global-refugee-crisis/402718/#note-405247-the-cost-of-resettling-a-syrian-refugee-in-the-us).

10. See, for example, Randy Capps and Michael Fix, "Ten Facts about U.S. Refugee Settlement," Migration Policy Institute Fact Sheet, October 2015 (www.migrationpolicy.org/research/ten-facts-about-us-refugee-resettlement.)

11. Michael O'Hanlon, "Deconstructing the Syria Nightmare," *National Interest,* October 22, 2015 (www.nationalinterest.org/feature/deconstructing-the-syria-nightmare-14108?page=4), and "Deconstructing Syria: A New Strategy for America's Most Hopeless War," *Order from Chaos* (blog), June 30, 2015 (www.brookings.edu/blogs/order-from-chaos/posts/2015/06/30-deconstructing-syria-ohanlon).

12. David Ignatius, "The Big Hole in Obama's Islamic State Strategy," *Washington Post,* December 7, 2015 (www.washingtonpost.com/opinions/the-big-hole-in-obamas-islamic-state-strategy/2015/12/07/04ce2d16-9d01-11e5-bce4-708fe33e3288_story.html).

13. Brookings-Bern Project on Internal Displacement, *Addressing Internal Displacement in Peace Processes, Peace Agreements and Peace-Building*, Brookings Institution, September 2007 (www.brookings.edu/research/reports/2007/09/peaceprocesses).

14. Elizabeth Ferris and Sanjula Weerasinghe, *Security Council, Internal Displacement, and Protection: Recommendations for Strengthening Action through Resolutions*, Brookings-LSE Project on Internal Displacement, September 2011 (www.brookings.edu/research/reports/2011/09/security-council-resolutions-ferris).

15. World Bank, "Turkey's Response to the Syrian Refugees Crisis and the Road Ahead," December 2015, p. 2 (www-wds.worldbank.org/external/default/WDSContentServer/WDSP/IB

/2015/12/21/090224b083ed7485/1_0/Rendered/PDF/Turkey0s0
respo0s0and0the0road0ahead.pdf).

16. Neils Harild, Asger Christensen, and Roger Zetter, "Sustainable Refugee Return: Triggers, constraints and lessons on addressing the development challenges of forced displacement," *Global Program on Forced Displacement Issue Series of The World Bank Group*, August 2015 (www-wds.worldbank.org/external/default/WDS ContentServer/WDSP/IB/2015/09/22/090224b0830f4d16/1_0/ Rendered/PDF/Sustainable0re00forced0displacement.pdf).

17. Liz Sly, "The Ruins of Kobane: What One Small Town Says about the Destruction of Syria," *Washington Post*, November 13, 2015 (www.washingtonpost.com/sf/world/2015/11/13/kobane/).

18. See resources on transitional justice and displacement available at www.brookings.edu/about/projects/idp/durable-solu tions-to-displacement/transitional-justice.

19. For further discussion of accountability in Syria, see Nick Robins-Early, "How Will Syria's Assad Be Held Accountable for Crimes against Humanity?," *Huffington Post*, March 28, 2015 (www. huffingtonpost.com/2015/03/28/syria-war-crimes_n_6950660. html). Also see the Syria Accountability Project at http://syria accountability.org/.

20. UN Human Rights Council, "Report of the Independent International Commission of Inquiry on the Syrian Arab Republic," A/HRC/30/48, August 13, 2015 (www.ohchr.org/EN/ HRBodies/HRC/IICISyria/Pages/IndependentInternational-Commission.aspx), p. 21.

21. Dawn Chatty and Nisrine Mansour, "Unlocking Protracted Displacement: An Iraqi Case Study," *Refugee Studies Quarterly* 30, no. 4 (November 3, 2011), p. 7 (http://rsq.oxfordjournals.org/con tent/30/4/50.abstract).

22. Katy Long, *From Refugee to Migrant? Labor Mobility's Protection Potential* (Washington: Migration Policy Institute, May 2015) (www.migrationpolicy.org/research/refugee-migrant-labor-mobilitys-protection-potential).

23. Elizabeth G. Ferris, *The Politics of Protection: The Limits of Humanitarian Action* (Brookings, 2011).

24. "G-20 Leaders' Communique Antalya Summit, Novem-

ber 15-16, 2015," Council of the European Council press releases and statements, November 16, 2015 (www.consilium.europa. eu/en/press/press-releases/2015/11/16-g20-summit-antalya-communique/).

25. Alexander Betts and Jean-François Durieux, "Convention Plus as a Norm-Setting Exercise," *Journal of Refugee Studies* 20, no. 3 (2007): 509–35; and Astri Suhrke, "Burden-Sharing during Refugee Emergencies: The Logic of Collective versus National Action," *Journal of Refugee Studies* 11, no. 4 (1998): 396–415.

26. A typical reaction is captured by this statement: "The attitude of developed states can be summarized as 'Open the eastern borders to the full extent, but shut down your western borders tightly,'" in M. Murat Erdoğan and Can Ünver, "Perspectives, Expectations and Suggestions of the Turkish Business Sector on Syrians in Turkey," Turkish Confederation of Employer Associations, December 2015, p. 34 (https://mmuraterdogan.files.wordpress. com/2016/01/syrians-eng-mme.pdf).

27. Tim Arango, "Turkey Moves to Clamp down on Border, Long a Revolving Door," *New York Times,* December 22, 2015 (www.nytimes.com/2015/12/23/world/europe/turkey-border-refugees.html?smid=nytcore-iphone-share&smprod=nytcore-iphone&_r=0).

28. Melih Aslan, "Migrants Fleeing Syria Encounter a Life of Detention in Turkey," *Washington Post,* December 27, 2015 (www. washingtonpost.com/world/migrants-fleeing-syria-encounter-a-life-of-detention-in-turkey/2015/12/27/3f63ce4c-acdb-11e5-9ab0-884d1cc4b33e_story.html), and "Turkey: Syrians Pushed Back at the Border," Human Rights Watch, November 23, 2015 (www. hrw.org/news/2015/11/23/turkey-syrians-pushed-back-border).

29. Alexander Betts, "Comprehensive Plans of Action: Insights from CIREFCA and the Indochinese CPA," *New Issues in Refugee Research*, Working Paper No. 120, UNHCR, January 2006 (www. unhcr.org/43eb6a152.html); and W. Courtland Robinson, "The Comprehensive Plan of Action for Indochinese Refugees, 1989–1997: Sharing the Burden and Passing the Buck," *Journal of Refugee Studies* 17, no. 3 (2004): 319–33.

30. For example, see "Joint Announcement from the United

Kingdom, Germany, Norway, Kuwait, and the United Nations on the Syrian Donors Conference 2016," UK Prime Minister's Office, press releases, November 16, 2015 (www.gov.uk/government/news/syria-donors-conference-2016-joint-announcement).   Also see Filippo Dionigi, "Do We Need a Regional Compact for Refugee Protection in the Middle East?," London School of Economics Middle East Centre blog (http://blogs.lse.ac.uk/mec/2015/10/30/do-we-need-a-regional-compact-for-refugee-protection-in-the-middle-east/).

31. Countries sending the most refugees are Syria, Afghanistan, Somalia, Sudan, Eritrea (almost half of the population is Muslim), and Iraq. Countries receiving the most refugees are Turkey, Pakistan, Lebanon, Iran, Jordan, and Sudan (www.unhcr.org/56701b969.html), pp. 6–7.

32. "Joint Statement of the Ministerial Meeting of Syria Bordering Countries organized by the United Nations High Commissioner for Refugees," September 4, 2013 (www.mfa.gov.tr/joint-statement-of-the-ministerial-meeting-of-syria-bordering-countries-organized-by-the-united-nations-high-commissioner-for-refugees_-4-september-2013.en.mfa); and "Ministerial Coordination Meeting of Major Host Countries for Syrian Refugees," January 17, 2014 (www.mfa.gov.tr/ministerial-coordination-meet ing-of-major-host-countries-for-syrian-refugees_-17-january-2013_-sanliurfa.en.mfa). No joint statement appears to have been adopted at the end of the meeting in May 2014. The meeting in May 2014 was reported by Mehmet Nayir, "Davutoğlu: No One Will Accept the Legitimacy of Syrian Presidential Elections," *Daily Sabah*, May 4, 2014, (www.dailysabah.com/nation/2014/05/05/davutoglu-no-one-will-accept-the-legitimacy-of-syrian-presidential-elections).

33. "Remarks by World Bank Group President Jim Yong Kim at the MENA Stakeholders Event," October 10, 2015 (www.worldbank.org/en/news/speech/2015/10/10/world-bank-group-president-jim-yong-kim-mena-stakeholders-event)

34. For more information, please refer to the alliance website: www.endingdisplacement.org/.

35. This idea is more explicitly spelled out in Filippo Dionigi,

"Do We Need a Regional Compact for Refugee Protection in the Middle East?"

36. Ishaan Tharoor, "Canada Races Ahead of the US in Bid to Resettle Syrian Refugees," *Washington Post,* November 25, 2015 (www.washingtonpost.com/news/worldviews/wp/2015/11/25/canada-races-ahead-of-the-u-s-in-bid-to-resettle-syrian-refugees/).

37. Austin Ramzy, "Tony Abbott Says Australia Will Accept 12,000 More Refugees," *New York Times,* September 9, 2015 (www.nytimes.com/2015/09/10/world/asia/australia-to-accept-additional-12000-refugees-from-iraq-and-syria.html?_r=0).

38. UNHCR, "Resettlement and Other Forms of Legal Admission for Syrian Refugees," December 11, 2015 (www.unhcr.org/52b2febafc5.pdf).

39. "Fact and Figures: Syria Refugee Crisis & International Resettlement," Amnesty International, December 5, 2014 (www.amnesty.org/en/latest/news/2014/12/facts-figures-syria-refugee-crisis-international-resettlement/). For a detailed empirical study of the question, see "A Note on Syrian Refugees in the Gulf," Gulf Labour Markets and Migration (http://gulfmigration.eu/media/pubs/exno/GLMM_EN_2015_11.pdf).

40. Luay al-Khatteeb, "The Gulf States Should Do More for Syrian Refugees," *Markaz* (blog), September 30, 2015 (www.brookings.edu/blogs/markaz/posts/2015/09/30-gulf-states-syrian-refugees-alkhateeb).

41. See World Bank's overview on the Middle East and North Africa region (www.worldbank.org/en/region/mena/overview#2).

42. Omer Karasapan, "Conflict and Development: the World Bank Group's New Strategy for the Middle East and North Africa Region," *Voices and Views* (blog), October 13, 2015 (http://blogs.worldbank.org/arabvoices/conflict-and-development-world-bank-group-new-strategy-mena).

43. World Bank, "New Joint Initiative to Mobilize Additional Support for Refugees, Recovery and Reconstruction in the Middle East and North Africa," October 10, 2015 (www.worldbank.org/en/news/press-release/2015/10/10/new-joint-initiative-to-mobilize-additional-support-for-refugees-in-the-middle-east-and-north-africa).

44. See, for example, the United States Institute of Peace's earlier work around "the day after" (www.usip.org/the-day-after-project) and the Atlantic Council's Task Force on US Policy toward Syria: "Albright and Hadley to Lead Atlantic Council's Task Force on US Strategy for the Middle East," Atlantic Council (www.atlanticcouncil.org/news/press-releases/bright-and-hadley-to-lead-atlantic-council-task-force-on-us-strategy-for-the-middle-east).

45. See "Brookings' Bruce Riedel Doubts the Nation-State of Syria Will Exist in Five Years," Bloomberg Politics, December 29, 2015 (www.bloomberg.com/politics/videos/2015-12-29/i-doubt-syria-will-exist-in-5-years-bruce-riedel). Also see Philip Gordon, James Dobbins, and Jeff Martini, "A Realistic Plan for Syria Needs to Begin with an Immediate Ceasefire," *Washington Post*, December 17, 2015 (www.washingtonpost.com/opinions/a-realistic-peace-plan-for-syria/2015/12/17/1a004eca-a414-11e5-ad3f-991ce3374e23_story.html). This idea of an eventual partition of Syria, in effect ratifying the present situation, was repeatedly mentioned by a variety of actors during field research conducted by the authors in the region in mid-2015.

46. Harriet Grant, "UN Agencies 'Broke and Failing' in Face of Ever-Growing Refugee Crisis," *The Guardian*, September 6, 2015 (available at www.unhcr.org/cgi-bin/texis/vtx/refdaily?pass=52fc6fbd5&id=55ed22505).

47. Christian Els and Nils Carstensen, "Funding of Local and National Humanitarian Actors," *Local to Global Protection*, May 2015, p. 3 (www.local2global.info/wp content/uploads/l2gp_local_funding_final_250515.pdf).

48. Michael Barnett and Peter Walker, "Regime Change for Humanitarian Aid: How to Make Relief More Accountable," *Foreign Affairs*, July/August 2015 (www.foreignaffairs.com/articles/2015-06-16/regime-change-humanitarian-aid). Also see United Nations Office for the Coordination of Humanitarian Affairs, "Restoring Humanity: Global Voices Call for Action. Synthesis Report of the Consultation Process for the World Humanitarian Summit," 2015 (www.worldhumanitariansummit.org/bitcache/e29bc4269edb7eaeceb5169a8f41275327a701c8?vid=555558&disposition=inline&op=view).

Index

Ukraine, 2

Unemployment, 59–60, 96. *See also* Jobs

UNICEF, 54, 63, 135

United Kingdom, 16, 65–66, 100, 105

United Nations: Conciliation Commission for Palestine, 8–9; humanitarian aid from, 91; on humanitarian aid to Iraq, 24; on IDPs, 72; Independent Commission of Inquiry on Syria, 18, 81; peacekeeping operations, 110. *See also* General Assembly; Security Council; *specific offices and programs*

United Nations Development Program (UNDP), 26

United Nations High Commissioner for Refugees (UNHCR): humanitarian aid from, 91; IDPs and, 72, 75; Iraqi refugees and, 11, 81; Jordan and, 38, 49; Kurdish refugees and, 87; mandate for, 7; New Global Approach for Syria and, 131, 132, 135, 138, 139; Palestinian refugees and, 9; resettlement and, 66; role of, 35–36; Syrian refugees and, 128–29; Turkey and, 48, 54

United Nations Office for the

Coordination of Humanitarian Affairs. *See* Office for the Coordination of Humanitarian Affairs, UN (OCHA).

United Nations Relief and Works Agency (UNRWA), 8, 79, 81

United States: humanitarian aid from, 100; Iraqi refugees resettled in, 12; military intervention against ISIS, 85–86; New Global Approach for Syria and, 132–33; opposition forces supported by, 16; public opinion on refugees in, 69–70, 113–14; refugee assistance funding from, 65–66; resettlement of refugees in, 122; safe zones and, 105

United States Agency for International Development, 76

Uppsala Conflict Data Program, 3

Uruguay, 132

Vienna process, 117

Vietnam, 128

Vocational training, 54

Wahid al-Balous, 22

War crimes, 15, 25, 73–74, 117–18